MEET THESE MEN

CLOVIS G. CHAPPELL

MEET THESE MEN

ABINGDON PRESS
New York • Nashville

MEET THESE MEN

Library of Congress Catalog Card Number: 56-6354

B

SET UP, PRINTED, AND BOUND BY THE PARTHENON PRESS, AT NASHVILLE, TENNESSEE, UNITED STATES OF AMERICA

To my grandson

DAVID

CONTENTS

The Man Who

1

The Man Who Was Independent

Be dependent on nobody.
I Thess. 4:12

✣✣✣✣✣✣✣✣✣✣✣✣✣✣✣✣✣✣✣✣✣✣✣✣✣✣✣✣✣✣✣✣✣✣✣✣✣✣

"Be dependent on nobody." Here is a word with a universal appeal. Everybody admires independence. Sometime ago I saw a young mother trying to lead her small boy who was just learning to walk. It happened that the little chap did not wish to be led. Therefore, he snatched loose from his mother and went off on his own. He had not gone ten feet until down he went. His mother hurried to pick him up, but before she reached him he was gone again. Then down he went again, then up again and down again. At last, when he came to the only muddy place in the road, down he went once more, splashing his clean dress, his clean face, and even his mother's temper.

"What are you going to do next?" she asked in indignation. With a grin on his muddy little face he answered, "I am going to get up." At once my hat was off to him. I had to admire his independence.

A certain city where I was once pastor was dominated by a gangster government. A keen and capable young lawyer, the teacher of the men's Bible class in his church, had the courage to run for a minor office in that city, in opposition to the gangsters. He won, and almost everybody applauded. But a year or two later he was offered a larger office by the opposition. He sold out. Today he is still in a rather prominent position but is about as influential as a wax figure in a show window. He has even taken to drink, seeking thereby, I feel sure, to lessen the pain of his hurt self-respect. Even his enemies regard him with a measure of pity and contempt. His once vital independence is as dead as a mummy.

We admire independence in the pulpit. In truth, if the prophet loses his independence, he ceases to be a prophet. A few years ago I knew a minister who was pastor of one of our largest churches. There was a gentleman in his church and on his official board whose contribution to the budget was unusually large. Now it came to pass that when this pastor announced a service in the interest of prohibition, this generous gentleman at once sent him an urgent letter of protest. He declared that since the liquor question was purely political it had no place in the pulpit. That pastor saw this large contribution, which was much needed, vanishing into thin air. In spite of that fact he wrote a letter after this fashion.

"My dear Friend: I see from your letter that you are a convinced wet. It happens that I am a convinced dry. The only way I know to keep my self-respect and to keep your respect for me is to act like what I am. Therefore, the meeting will go on as per schedule."

That pastor received a very gracious letter from his wet friend. Not only so, but he continued to receive his large contribution. This was not the case, I am sure, because that wet friend had come to agree with his minister.

It was rather because he was compelled to admire and respect his independence in spite of his inability to agree.

Now since everybody admires independence, everybody would like to be independent. Some desire it so much that they are willing to make almost any sacrifice in order to win it. That is true of peoples and nations. It is perhaps truer at this moment than at any other time in history. The underprivileged nations are today demanding the right to manage their own affairs and make their own mistakes. Woe unto the privileged if they fail to recognize and yield to this passion! In my opinion it is this longing for independence, even above all the other causes, that will at last spell the doom of Communism.

As we long and struggle for independence as a group, so we do as individuals. Sometimes we struggle foolishly and sometimes wisely. Be that as it may, the struggle still goes on. I read some time ago of a brilliant young businessman who was making money rapidly. A wise old friend asked him what was his ambition.

"I want to be worth a million dollars," was his reply.

"Why so?" his friend continued.

This was the answer, "So I can tell the other fellow to go to hell." That is not as brutal as it sounds. The young chap meant only that it was his ambition to become rich enough to be absolutely independent. Here, then, is a virtue which everyone admires and for which everyone longs.

I

Now Paul had won this prize. He was in the finest sense independent. What, then, had he achieved?

1. He was independent of things. Of course, this great preacher and saint had to have food to eat and clothing to wear even as you and I. But though he declared that those who preached the gospel had a right to live off the gospel, he himself never claimed that right. On the contrary, he told the church at Corinth that he would rather die than to give up the privilege of paying his own way. He delighted in displaying his work-worn hands. Even when his dear church at Philippi sent him a gift, though that gift made his heart fairly sing for joy, his gladness was for the enrichment that such a winsome deed would bring to the givers rather than to himself, the receiver. In fact, he felt that in sober honesty he must tell his friends that, while their gift was sweet with the very perfume of heaven, yet it was not necessary. He could have managed without it. He had learned in whatsoever state he was therewith to be content.

It is well to bear in mind, however, that in refusing a salary Paul was not merely seeking to relieve his converts and thus make the way of Christ easy. He would have been the first to agree that no greater calamity can come to a church than to possess a cheap faith. Such would be as deadly as a hydrogen bomb. No church can live unless the shadow of the cross falls in some measure upon the checkbooks of those who belong to it. Therefore, though he refused to ask money for himself, he was utterly shameless in asking for it in order to help others. But personally he was independent in his relation to things.

2. He was independent as an apostle. All the other apostles had known Jesus in the flesh. All but one of them,

the one chosen by lot, had been called by their Lord by word of mouth. It was not so with Paul. Yet this did not give him a sense either of inferiority or of dependence upon his fellow apostles. He declared that he himself had seen Jesus Christ our Lord. He declared further that since he had been personally called and commissioned by the risen Lord he was not one whit behind the chiefest of the apostles. He was eager that they be in agreement with him. Be that as it may, this independent man had a gospel all his own. Possessed by that gospel, he largely made the channels in which the theological thought of the centuries has flowed.

3. Then he was independent with regard to his fellows. He loved deeply and widely. His heart was a veritable house of many mansions. He numbered all sorts of people among his friends. He also had a wide and varied assortment of enemies. But in the presence of all these he was grandly independent.

He was independent in the face of his foes. He loved the approval of his fellows as we all do. However, he met criticism and opposition with a fine manliness. After he had spent a night in jail in Philippi, the authorities sent word to his jailer that he might now be set at liberty. A man of lesser independence would have gone gladly. But not Paul. Rather, he sent word back, "They have beaten us publicly, uncondemned, men who are Roman citizens, and have thrown us into prison; and do they now cast us out secretly? No! let them come themselves and take us out." He was too independent to bear such outrage without protest.

If Paul was independent in the face of imprisonment, he was equally independent in the presence of threatened death. "If . . . I . . . have committed anything for which I deserve to die," he declared on one occasion, "I do not seek to escape death." Then again he affirmed that while at his first trial no man stood with him, yet the Lord had stood by and had given him inward strength. As a result, though knowing that he was on the point of being sacrificed, he faced the ordeal without a whine. He was independent in the presence of his foes.

What is often more difficult, he was independent also of his friends. He deeply loved these friends, but he was neither dominated nor swerved from his course by them. That was a beautiful oneness that the church was enjoying at Antioch. Jews and Gentiles were in brotherly love working and living together. But that oneness was shattered by the coming of messengers from Jerusalem. Under their pressure even such great souls as Barnabas and Simon Peter surrendered and went over to the conservatives. But not Paul. He not only held his ground but he boldly rebuked his dear brethren of the ministry, though it must have cost him heavily.

Perhaps even a sharper test came when certain friends, sure that his proposed visit to Jerusalem would result in tragedy, sought to dissuade him from his purpose. They all but laid violent hands on him as they sought with tenderness and tears to persuade him to play it safe. How hard it must have been for a sensitive soul like Paul to resist such an appeal. Yet he did resist it. Half desperately he turned upon them with these words: "What are you doing, weeping and breaking my heart? For I am ready not only to be imprisoned but even to die at Jerusalem for the name of the Lord Jesus." Here, then, is a man who was grandly independent.

II

How did he get that way?

Let it be said at once that he did not win by casting off all restraint. Independence is a fine virtue. But, like many another virtue, when pushed too far it becomes a vice. It is wise to be cautious, but caution can easily degenerate into cowardice. To conserve is a virtue, but pushed too far it becomes that ghastly sin of miserliness. Even so, while independence is good, if pushed too far it results in disaster.

This is true in the state. During the days of the judges personal liberty seems to have reached its climax. The author of the book says "every man did what was right in his own eyes." Everybody learned complete independence. What a grand day in which to live! No, it was not grand at all. Such independence resulted in anarchy and a complete loss of freedom. The very roadways grew up because men no longer dared to travel them. When everybody in a state does just as he pleases, everybody becomes in a measure a slave.

Complete independence would wreck the home. I admired the little chap who snatched loose from his mother and went out on his own. But if he continues that course without any kind of restraint, he is likely to wreck himself and to break his mother's heart. When husbands and wives become independent of each other, their marriage goes upon the rocks. When parents become independent of their children, they destroy them through their neglect. Complete independence in the home would mean complete disaster.

It is even so in our relations one with another. What has blackened the reputation of the priest and the Levite? Not the fact that they joined the robbers in their attack upon a certain helpless traveler. They simply said of the wounded man, "He is none of my business. I cannot be bothered." But every man is my business. I am also the business of everyone else. We are bound up in a bundle of life with each other. To seek merely to save my own life is surely to lose it.

Nobody recognized this more clearly than did this independent man Paul. Therefore, he wrote, "Though I am free from all men, I have made myself a slave to all." "Who is weak," he questioned, "and I am not weak? Who is made to fall, and I am not indignant?" Thus he shouldered the burdens of high and the low, rich and the poor. Thus he bled through the wounds of every sufferer and wept through the tears of every lonely heart. His independence, therefore, was not absolute.

What, then, was his secret? His independence was born of his utter dependence upon God. Independence is essentially a religious question. Independence toward God is the fountain source of all sin. When the prodigal left home, he was not seeking to wreck himself. He was not seeking to hurt his father. He was only seeking to be independent of his father. Independence toward God has in it the seed of all tragedy. But dependence upon him has in it the possibilities of all independence. It was Paul's utter dependence upon God that enabled him to be independent in every other relationship. It enabled him to

> meet with Triumph and Disaster
> And treat those two imposters just the same.

Naturally this type of independence reached its climax in Jesus. How grandly independent he was! There was never a compromise, never an appeal to the gallery. When he stood defenseless before Pilate, he towered above him as Pikes Peak above an anthill. What was the matter with this Roman official? He lacked independence. Therefore, when somebody shouted from the crowd, "If you release this man, you are not Caesar's friend," Pilate went hot and cold and flung the accused to the wolves. This he did because he was utterly dependent upon Caesar.

But Jesus was dependent only upon God. This was so complete that he declared, "I can do nothing on my own authority." That gave him an independence so staggeringly magnificent that he stepped across the threshold of death declaring in spite of his seeming failure, "I have overcome the world."

Everybody admires independence. Everybody struggles in some measure for it. It is a God-given longing. But nobody can attain it by traveling the road of rebellion. We can only reach that high goal by a complete dependence upon God. Depending fully upon him, we can fulfill this great word "Be dependent on nobody."

2

The Man Who Was No Good

Formerly he was useless.
Philem. 1:11

A great many years ago in the city of Colossae there lived a young chap who saw his visions and dreamed his dreams even as you and I. But he felt himself held back from the big game of life because he wore a chain. Tradition says that he had been sold into slavery for debt. It may have been for his own debt that he had mortgaged his tomorrow to his today. Anyway, he stood on the sideline and watched the game played and was unable to take part in it, until he became so wretched that he decided to make a break for liberty.

So one night he slipped out of the slaves' quarters and into his master's quarters, where he armed himself with his master's gold. Thus armed, he stole out through the window, hugged the deepest shadows, and made for the open country. Then he hurried to hide himself in the city of Ephesus. But not feeling safe there, he made his way into that great human jungle of antiquity called Rome, where all sorts of human vermin could home and sting in comparative safety. There he looked upon the big city that ruled the world. He saw how right was trodden under foot of might and how splendor rode hard on the boney shoulders of squalor. Thus he perhaps came to look on life with cynical eyes.

Then I imagine that one day a denizen of the underworld like himself said, "By the way, Onesimus, there's going to be a show in the arena tonight. I wonder if you would like to go?"

"I would like to well enough," the young man answered. "But you see, I am a runaway slave. I am afraid of the police."

"Yes, I know," urged his tempter, "but this is going to be a very interesting show, one you can't afford to miss. They have some Christians over there who have been eating three meals a day. They also have some lions that haven't had a bite to eat for a week. They are going to put the two together in the arena for a vaudeville act. It will be quite exciting."

"All right," the young chap answered bitterly. "Since my master is a Christian, I'll go and see a few of them eaten just out of respect for him." So he went to the show.

Now, the bloody business over, as he was coming away I imagine that there walked at his side a man out of whose eyes looked the peace of a great discovery. He watched this haunted young man rather wistfully. Then to test him he made on the pavement the sign of a fish which was a password among the early Christians. They used the word "fish" because of its spelling in Greek. It meant to them, "Jesus Christ, Son of God, Savior."

The young chap understood at once, and it half angered him. "No, no," he replied. "Not a Christian, not if I know myself."

"Well," said his questioner, "I am sorry you are not. It has meant everything to me. But I have a friend in town I would be glad for you to meet. He's a much-traveled man. His feet mark all Roman roads. He's a fighting man. There isn't a square inch on his body that doesn't wear a scar. He's a much-thoughted man. You could "rub enough learning off his coat sleeve to make you a scholar." I am sorry to tell you that he is in jail just at this time. But if you care to meet him, I will be glad to introduce you."

Therefore, a few days later this runaway slave, partly because he was homesick, but more because he was heart-sick, went to see this man who since has become an acquaintance of all centuries. His friends knew him simply as Brother Paul. We know him as St. Paul. Soon, with a skill that amounted to inspired genius, Paul introduced this slave to Jesus Christ and he became a Christian.

A little later, in proof of the genuineness of his Christianity, I imagine that he showed up again at the jail. "Brother Paul," he said, "I am not what you think I am. I stole the money with which I came to Rome. Now that I have been converted, don't you think I ought to go back and straighten matters up?"

Paul looked at him tenderly and said, "Yes, I think that would be fine. But have you remembered that if you go back you might have to remain a slave the rest of yuor life?"

"Yes," he replied, "I have thought of that, but I had

rather wear a ball and chain round my ankle than to wear one round my conscience."

"Good," the preacher answered. "But tell me your master's name. I might write him a letter that would help you."

"His name is Philemon," the slave answered. "He lives in Colossae."

"Oh," said the preacher, "I know him." Then, having written a brief note, he gave that note to this chap who had been notoriously no good. He gave it to a slave who had a thousand opportunities to duck down some back alley and forget it all. But this he refused to do. Therefore, we can still read that letter in an old book if we are so minded. It is so shot through with those values that outlast the ages that the world simply could not let it be lost.

This so beautifully tender and so tenderly beautiful letter reaches its climax in these words: "I appeal to you for my child, Onesimus, whose father I have become in my imprisonment. (Formerly he was useless to you, but now he is indeed useful to you and to me.)"

"That is," said Paul, "I got hold of a young chap over here the other day who was no good. He was worth nothing to himself; he was worth nothing to his friends; he was worth nothing to society. I am sending him back. He will count for something today and tomorrow because he has met me and through me he has met Jesus Christ."

Now when Paul said that, he justified his right to his place in the sun. Indeed, the first question we ask about any creature or thing is this: What is it for? If it cannot give a reason for itself in terms of service, we reserve the right to junk it. Every man is expected to help make the useless into the useful or make what is already useful into something of greater usefulness. That is what life is for.

I

Now this lifting of the lower into the higher is a fascinating task. Some years ago I visited Sleepy Hollow cemetery in Concord, Massachusetts. Of course, I was interested in the graves of Louisa May Alcott and Nathaniel Hawthorne and other notables who are buried there. But there was the grave of another, not nearly so well known, that interested me almost as much as these. This man was out walking in the forest years ago when he met a little winter grape. That grape was so insignificant that if it had been erased from the map nobody would have seriously missed it. But this man saw the little worthless thing and believed in it. He began to cultivate it, and when he left it, it was the Concord grape that we know today.

Not so long ago, if you had been walking in the fields with a little child, and that child had started to pluck a small berrylike thing growing at your feet, you would have said, "No, don't do that. That is a love apple. It is poisonous." But another man came and saw that despised love apple and believed in it and began to cultivate it. Thus it became the luscious tomato that we know today.

Not so many years ago a man named Luther Burbank died in the West. Luther Burbank declared, "Every weed is a possible flower." What amazing confidence he had in the vegetable kingdom. His attitude was: "The only reason this old burweed hasn't its hands full of beauty instead of cocklebUrs is because nobody has cared to give it a chance." In proof of the genuineness of his contention, one day he met a cactus, fell in love with it, and began at once to transform it. So successful was he that at last this cactus put down all its swords and spears and bayonets to fill its hands with flowers. Today when we meet it, we no longer gather our garments about us lest it should touch us, but we long to wear its colorful beauty over our hearts. Thus he found a foe and made it into a friend.

But in this work of lifting the lower into the higher our Lord is the supreme artist. Whatever he touches, he touches to transform. In his fellowship fluctuating Simon becomes a rock; demon-possessed Mary of Magdala becomes the first to herald the Resurrection; and Saul, the greatest menace of the early church, is changed into its greatest missionary. Too often we seek to escape him in the fear that he has come to wrench some precious value out of our hands. But always he comes that we may have life and have it in abundance.

II

How, then, are we to go about this fascinating task that is everybody's high privilege and that constitutes the very poetry of living?

A good place to begin is with ourselves. If we are to do the best for others, we must become our best. Years ago I knew a boy, the youngest of a large family, who had no interest in his educational opportunities. According to his own statement he never expected to learn to read. He thought that such achievement was at once useless and sissy. Naturally he was the despair of the family. His older brothers and sisters nicknamed him "Muttonhead." But he accepted it with utter complacency, being quite satisfied with himself.

Then something happened. A beautiful little girl from the city, two years younger than himself, came to visit in his backwoods home. She came out of a world of culture and of books. She knew nothing of the world of country life in which Muttonhead lived. Therefore, in his own field, he was her master. He at once began to show her his prowess with the horses and the cattle. He was a good rider. He was equally at home on the back of a horse or of a yearling calf. As he thus put on one skillful stunt after another, her eyes fairly sparkled with amazed admiration. "You are wonderful," she would exclaim to his great delight.

In the warmth of such admiration he grew and grew and grew until he became Hercules and Samson and Goliath, all bound up in one big package. But it was too good to last. One morning this lovely little girl failed to come down to breakfast. Instead, she sent for Muttonhead. When he arrived, she said with confidence, "I have sent for you to read me a story."

"What?" he answered in consternation. "You want me to read you a story?"

"Yes," she said, handing him a book opened at the story she desired to hear.

That was fatal. But Muttonhead did not at once make

an abject surrender. "I can't read that," he bluffed," "I read in the Fourth Reader."

"All right," she agreed sweetly. "Read me a story from that." So he went and actually found the book and came back with it like an ox to the slaughter. When he handed it to her, she picked out the story that she wished to hear. But again he failed. At that she laughed at him, but that did not move him. He had had that before. Then all the laughter went out of her eyes and they filled up with an amazed pity. "Why," she said, "you ought to be in the First Reader."

What a humiliation! He could not fail to see that she was actually sorry for him. He found her pity all the more painful because he had just been experiencing the thrill of being a hero. So deeply did it jar him that he said to himself and to no other, "Some day I am going to know as much as you." Even to him it seemed a rash resolve, but he began at once to put it into effect.

Naturally nobody quite understood why this backward boy made about four grades the next year. Then some five or six years later, when he was coming home from school, he passed through the city where this girl was then living, a beautiful young woman. He went to call on her. About leaving time she picked up a Latin book and said, "My examination is tomorrow. I wonder if you would read this passage for me."

"Certainly, my dear," he answered. Then, having read it, he got his hat and slipped out into the night. When he found himself on the street alone, he almost broke his arm, patting himself on the back.

If we are to become our best, we must not only work, but we must work in the power of a vital religious faith. God needs us and gives to everyone his work. There is something unique about you. Since he knows you and what you are capable of becoming, it is only good sense to realize that you can never become your best apart from him. Whatever he touches, he touches to transfigure and to enrich. It is God and God alone who can bring us to our highest possibilities.

This is how life for Onesimus long ago took on a new departure. Having accepted Jesus Christ as his Savior and Lord, he dared to go back to his former master. He dared the danger of throwing away the freedom he had won by coming to Rome. He dared to run the risk of remaining a slave to the end of his days. I can imagine that if I as a pagan friend had met him along the way, and he had told how, having won his freedom, he was now going out of loyalty to Jesus Christ to throw it all away, I might have thought him an utter fool.

But he was not a fool. He was very wise. He was wise even if it turned out that he actually was going back into a lifetime of slavery. He had already discovered that the true freedom is inside a man where chains of iron cannot touch it, and he would a thousand times rather have this freedom than what he had known as he skulked about the streets of Rome in bondage to a guilty conscience. The New Testament does not tell us what happened to Onesimus, and it is possible that he did remain a slave. After Philemon read this letter, I can imagine him saying, "Isn't that just like a preacher, meddling in things he doesn't know anything about! There's only one way to handle these slaves." In that case, however, I can further imagine him crumpling the little roll of papyrus and tossing it into the wastebasket. Since the letter did not end up in the wastebasket, but rather was treasured so much that is was saved for all later generations to read, it is easier to imagine Philemon living up to Paul's confidence that "you will do even more than I say." I believe he not only forgave Onesimus, and accepted him as a Christian brother, but gave him his freedom. Furthermore, seeing what sort of Christian Onesimus had already shown himself to be, I believe this young man would proceed to dedicate that freedom to carrying on the work of the man to whom he owed it.

Whether Onesimus actually became a minister of the gospel, what services he rendered, how many he led from bondage to freedom, it is impossible to say. But of one thing we may be sure: he has enriched in some measure all the subsequent centuries. At this very hour he is reaching from that long-gone yesterday to put into our hands this priceless letter. He is now telling us how we too may experience the transforming power of Christ. He is telling how, thus transformed, we may also lift the lower into the higher and change the useless into the useful. That task is the very poetry of living.

3

The Man Who Refused to Be Fired

Far be it from me that I should sin against the Lord by ceasing to pray for you. *I Sam. 12:23*

These are the words of Samuel. This great man was the first mountainous personality to appear in Israel after the death of Moses some three centuries before him. Through those drab years the story of Israel was one of relapse and recovery only to relapse again. The human landscape was monotonously flat. Naturally, therefore, we are at once thrilled and gladdened when we come upon a Pikes Peak personality like Samuel.

He is all the more thrilling because he takes us by surprise. The soil of the world into which he was born had far too little fertility to grow such a great soul. Not only was it shallow and lean, but it was parched by moral drought. Yet, in spite of the surrounding desert, it was the happy privilege of Samuel to be born in an oasis. That oasis was the arms of a mother of genuine consecration.

For years Samuel threatened to be the child that never was. He was longed for and waited for but failed to come. At last Hannah gave herself to definite and persistent prayer for his coming. Then one day he was born. His coming was the signal for the breaking of morning on the hills of his mother's heart. He was doubly dear. He was dear because of what he was in himself. He was also dear because he had been given in answer to prayer.

Because she had thus received her child from God, and realized that he had belonged to God before he had become her own, she wisely and gladly dedicated him to God. This she did in the early years of his life. Having herself trained him through his morning days, she then took him to the temple and put him in the care of the best man she knew, a priest named Eli. This good man was far from perfect. He made a tragic failure in the training of his own sons. But we can forgive him much because of his wisdom in dealing with this choice lad, Samuel.

For a time Samuel attended to his duties in the temple with only an inherited faith. Then one night God was able to speak to this well-trained lad personally. At first Samuel mistook the voice divine for that of his teacher. But Eli so interpreted the voice of God to the lad that he passed from a religion of hearsay into one of experience. He came to know God for himself.

Thus gladdened and strengthened by a personal awareness of God, having learned to listen to the divine voice, he became God's spokesman. We read that "all Israel from Dan to Beer-sheba knew that Samuel was established as a prophet of the Lord." Samuel thus became a revelation of God to his people both by what he was in himself and by what he said. Through him, as Moffatt translates it, "once more the Eternal was to be seen." In thus bringing to his people a sense of God he rendered them a superlative service.

Not only did Samuel become a prophet, but he became a judge. He was a kind of circuit judge who went over his district holding courts in various centers. Not only was he a judge, but, since Israel at that time was a theocracy, he was virtually a king. He was therefore a many-sided man, a great and inspired leader, especially fitted to serve his people in that difficult day.

It is evident that he discharged his duties with fidelity and ability. The people had not been so well off for centuries. But as is often the case, they did not realize how well off they were. Therefore, they demanded a change. While Samuel exercised near kingly power, he did not do so with kingly pomp and pageantry. Therefore, longing for a more colorful ruler, longing to be like the nations round about them, they fired Samuel in order to put a king in his place.

Of course, they had a good reason. Samuel, they pointed out, was old and gray. The situation required a younger man. Believe it or not, there is a natural antipathy between youth and age. Therefore, without his consent, they superannuated Samuel. He was not yet old enough to retire, but they doubtless told themselves that they were doing him a favor by thus taking the yoke from his work-worn neck and turning him out.

I

How did Samuel react to this?

It all but broke his heart. The fact that he knew that they had rejected God rather than himself did not lighten his grief but made it only the greater. This was the case because he really cared for his people. He longed to serve them because he was sure that they needed his service. Not only so, but he realized, in all humility, that he was the man of all the others best fitted for the task. After he was retired, though he was loyal to Saul and backed him in every possible way, he must have known that he towered above this tall king as a mountain above a molehill.

But, in my opinion, Samuel was not only grieved; he was genuinely indignant. He knew that he had been thrown aside without just cause. He could not help being outraged by such crass ingratitude. Though he was one of the best of men, pride was not yet utterly dead within his heart. Therefore, he was sorely tempted to mistake his wounded pride for the zeal of the Lord and to give up all further effort to serve.

"Far be it from me that I should sin against the Lord by ceasing to pray for you." Just why did he say that? I feel sure it was because this sin was exactly what he was most tempted to commit. "I have given these ingrates my best," he probably said to himself. "I have served them in every way possible. But it is now evident that they no longer care for my services. All right, they do not have to have them. Let them go their own way, and I will go mine. I can certainly get along without them as well as they can get along without me. Therefore, I am not going to try to serve them any more. I am not even going to continue to pray for them."

That is quite a human reaction. We have all had such a temptation. I once had in my church a man who as a member of the official board seemed to me to be making no contribution at all. But he was rather outstanding as a teacher of young men. His class was one of the best in our church school. Therefore, desiring that he give first attention to his teaching, I left him off the list of nominees for the board. Did he appreciate it? He did not. On the contrary, he was so indignant that he came to me saying that if he was not fit to be on the board neither was he fit to teach. Therefore, he was going to give up his class.

Knowing him to be a genuinely good man, I dared to give him this answer, "All right, if you can get away with it with your Lord and your own conscience, go ahead. Just tell God that, though you are making a real contribution as a teacher, you are going to quit because you are indignant at your pastor." I am happy to say that he did not quit.

No more did Samuel. Though he had been shut out of doing the task for which he was trained and for which he felt himself best fitted, he could not persuade himself that this gave him the right to do nothing at all. Because he could no longer serve in his chosen way, he felt that he should still serve in some way. Nor could he convince himself that the lack of appreciation on the part of his people gave him the right to fold his hands in utter idleness. He would certainly have preferred to continue the work of other years in an atmosphere of appreciation. But wanting these, he felt that he ought still to carry on. If other doors were shut, there was still one door open. That was the door of intercessory prayer. Therefore he said, "Far be it from me that I should sin against the Lord by ceasing to pray for you."

II

What came of this high resolve?

1. His decision to pray for others brought enrichment to his own life. Intercessory prayer helps the intercessor. Of course that is not its primary purpose. It is certainly one of its by-products. When I go fishing now and then in the river upon which I spent my boyhood, my primary purpose is to catch fish. Yet, even so, I catch much besides. I catch beauty. I catch the prattle of one of the loveliest streams that ever sang its way to the sea. I even catch tender memories of those who fished that same stream with me in youth's morning but are now on the banks of another river, the river of life.

When John Alden spoke to the woman he loved on behalf of his friend, he did not thereby lose her. He only won a roomier place in her gentle heart. Of all the forms of prayer that bring us into the divine fellowship and enable us to share the passion of our Lord, none I think is quite equal to intercessory prayer. It was this type of prayer to which Jesus gave himself in a peculiar way. Thus Samuel became a bigger man by praying for his people.

2. A second result of his praying for those who seemed not to desire his prayers was that he thus discovered new doors of opportunity and new power to enter those doors. That is generally the case. When youthful Isaiah came face to face with the appalling needs of his people, I dare

say he first looked about for some tall man to meet those needs. With his eyes fixed upon that man he probably prayed, "There he is. Send him." But since he was sincere, his prayer soon changed to this, "Here I am! Send me." Prayer is not a cheap way of getting God to do tasks that we are too cowardly or indifferent to undertake.

Across the years I have never been able to forget a certain service that was outstanding in its deadness. There was a little group of us in a large sanctuary, each one seeming desperately sorry that he was there. The scene was fairly parched by drought. Then that parched soil was whipped into a dust storm by a brother who, being called on to lead in prayer, pounded the pew and cried with the volume of a priest of Baal, "Lord, go out into the highways and hedges and compel them to come in." How shocking! That is just what the Lord told us to do. But here we were saying, "Lord, do it yourself; we are too busy."

Now it so happened that Samuel prayed in deep sincerity. Therefore, instead of having to suffer the boredom of idleness, he found that God was showing him other ways of serving. Relieved of his former work, he had time to listen to certain preachers of that day. As he listened, he was shocked by the fact that they were not so much preachers as howling dervishes. Therefore, he resolved to give them a chance to become real prophets. He began to establish what amounted to theological seminaries. Thus his work is blessing the world unto this day. I dare say he made a greater contribution after he was superannuated than he did before.

3. A third result of Samuel's praying was that he released the power of God upon those for whom he prayed. True prayer always has and always does release the power of God on a given situation or a given individual. The Bible abounds in victories wrought through such prayer. And the wonder is that the door of prayer remains open when all others are closed. Furthermore, it may be entered by anybody who is willing, whether old or young, rich or poor, cultured or ignorant, strong or ill. Some of the greatest victories of prayer have been wrought by invalids. This door, I repeat, is always open.

Look at this picture. When Sennacherib had his sword pressed against the heart of the weak city of Jersualem, there seemed no hope. His great army was only thirty-five miles away. Totally without military power, what could her king do? Just one thing, he could pray. That he did, and with this result:

> And the widows of Ashur are loud in their wail,
> And the idols are broke in the temple of Baal;
> And the might of the Gentile, unsmote by the sword,
> Hath melted like snow in the glance of the Lord.

It is a fact of history that Jerusalem was saved. "The long arm of coincidence" answers the unbeliever. "The strong arm of Almighty God" is the answer of faith.

When Simon Peter was in prison in Jerusalem, humanly speaking he did not have a chance in a million. But, in spite of prison walls, chains, and iron gates, he did escape. How? Here I think is the only sane explanation,

"But earnest prayer for him was made to God by the church." Unless the writers of both the Old and New Testaments are deceived, prayer does make it possible for God to do for us and through us what would otherwise be impossible.

"And so it was that all escaped to land." What a miracle! Who were these that escaped? They were a very mixed crowd of 276 souls. They were mainly pagans. They were alike in only one respect, in their despair as on board a wrecking vessel they faced certain disaster. Yet here they are, all safe ashore. What is the explanation? I am sure this is the answer. Paul had given himself to prayer for these nameless men. He had prayed until he had received this answer, "And lo, God has granted you all those who sail with you."

This is also the experience of many outside the Bible. Years ago I was conducting a revival under a tabernacle. One night after I had pronounced the benediction, a physician and his wife came forward and requested that I pray for their two sons, twenty-four and twenty-six years of age respectively. To this I readily agreed.

It so happened that at the moment a man who had known the physician and his wife across the years was standing at my side. It so happened further that this man was very learned in the school of prayer. Having heard the request of the physician and his wife, he exercised the privilege of a friend and broke in with this question: "Doctor, have you ever put yourself on the altar for your two boys?"

The physician was a bit puzzled at the question, as I was

myself. It was queer, old-fashioned language. So he answered, "I am not sure that I know what you mean."

"I mean this," was the reply. "If those were my boys, I would tell God here and now that I would not eat or sleep until he saved them." Then he added, "If you will take that vow, I will take it with you. I will pledge myself that I will not eat or sleep until your sons are saved."

I was inclined to step back out of the picture. I saw the water was a bit too deep for me. But the physician and his wife measured up. He answered, "I will not allow any man to do more for my boys than I am willing to do. Therefore we pledge ourselves, my wife and I, that we will not eat or sleep until our boys are saved."

Well, that was a bit startling. In spite of the fact that I had thought the conversation private, the news got round. Everybody who heard it knew that these three people were no longer engaged in target practice; they were now shooting to kill. The boys themselves were quite convinced of it, though they did not react in the same way.

The oldest son heard it with indignation. He declared with emphasis that he was not going to be driven into becoming a Christian. Therefore, though it was getting far into the night, he hitched his team to his farm wagon and, vowing profanely that he would not return until the meeting was over, set out for his ranch sixteen miles in the country.

The younger son went home and to bed. About one o'clock in the morning he waked to find two people kneeling at his bedside. "Dad, is that you?" he asked. "Mother, is that you?" At that he sprang out of bed, kneeled between them, and entered into the joy of a dedicated life. It was a thrill to see him present at the morning service next day.

Naturally we were impressed. But I was still wondering about the other son. He had gone to the country with the vow that he would not return until the meeting was over. With this in mind I began my sermon. A few minutes later I heard the rumble of a farm wagon. A little later still this older son came under the tabernacle. When I gave the invitation at the close of the service, he immediately came forward to make a public confession of his new-found faith.

What is the explanation? Personally I think that above all else it was a victory won by prayer. Such praying has and does still bring comfort, enrichment, power, and salvation. Therefore, I repeat, prayers offered in sincerity make it possible for God to do for us and in us and through us what he could do in no other way. Because this is true, let each of us say with Samuel, "Far be it from me that I should sin against the Lord by ceasing to pray."

4

The Man Who Was God's Friend

> Abram dwelt in the land of Canaan, while Lot dwelt among the cities of the valley and moved his tent as far as Sodom.
> *Gen. 13:12*

✣✣✣

This man, whose permanent name is Abraham, has a unique distinction. Three times over in the Bible he is called the friend of God. For this reason he is worth knowing. Perhaps we can get a clearer view of his face by looking at him as he stands beside his nephew Lot.

I

These two men, while having much in common, present a sharp contrast.

First, they are alike in that they were both religious men. They were both altar builders, both men of prayer. Though they lived a great many centuries ago, they were exceedingly modern. They would be almost as much at home in our day as they were in their own. If they were living in your city, they would perhaps belong to your church. In that case both would be on the official board. Abraham would be on the official board because he deserved to be and because you could not well run your church without him. Lot would be on the official board because he was kin to Abraham.

But in spite of the fact that they were both religious men, both good churchmen, as we should say today, yet they present a staggering contrast. In the richness of their own personal lives, in their influence upon their own families, in their influence upon the generation of which they were a part and upon all the generations that have followed since that day, they are as far apart as ghastly failure from radiant victory.

Lot gazes upon us across the far spaces of the years a pathetic ruin. The only message that comes to us from his dumb lips is, "Don't live your life as I lived mine. Don't throw yourself away as I threw myself away." In spite of his religion he was a tragic failure. Abraham, on the other hand, represents religion at its radiant best. He became God's friend. Even when the writers of the New Testament want to show us the beauty of faith, they hark back to this man who one day set out into the unknown because he had a strange conviction that God was going to do the impossible in and through him.

I am quite sure that his friends thought him a bit mad. They said of him, "He is a splendid fellow but a little off. He doesn't quite have his feet on the ground. Of course his mad dream will end in failure." For almost a century it looked as if they were right. But, in spite of the fact that the years seemed to bring him nothing but disappointment, he never gave up. He never turned back. He stood, leaning his shoulders against the promises of Almighty God, saying, "I know that God did speak to me.

I know that what God says must come to pass." This, say the writers of the New Testament, is religion at its radiant best.

II

Why this sharp contrast?

It was not because one was religious and the other was not. They were both religious. It was not because one was honest while the other was a crook. They were both honest. It was not that one was a drunkard while the other was sober. They were both sober. Why, I repeat, the difference? I think this is the answer: Both were religious, but one was only partially committed while the other was fully committed.

This very modern man, Lot, would have regarded himself today as a good churchman. He is spoken of in the New Testament as a righteous man. But this was his tragedy: While he was religious, his religion was never a vocation. It was always an avocation. It never became the biggest fact about him. When there came a test, when there came the necessity of a choice between his own interest and that of his Lord, his own interest won.

That is a piercing word we read in *The Screwtape Letters.* A chief devil is writing to his nephew, who is undertaking to wreck a certain human whom he calls his "patient." He writes in this fashion: "I hear your patient has become religious. Don't let that bother you unless he has become altogether religious. If he is only partially religious, he will be just as harmless and a lot more fun." What a keen thrust that is! With Abraham, on the other hand, his religion was the biggest fact about him. Since he was constantly walking in the direction that God was going, their roads ran together and they became friends. Thus, the prose of half committal was changed into the poetry of a full committal. This marked for them, as for us, the difference between partial defeat and joyful victory.

III

Now, the fact that we have read these two characters aright, I think, is indicated by the choices they made in an hour of crisis. A crisis, of course, never makes character. It only reveals it.

I was reading of a young couple, engaged to be married, who went together to a movie. While they were watching the picture, some excitable chap, thinking he saw a bit of smoke about the stage, shouted, "Fire!" At once this bridegroom-to-be, with the first law of nature strong upon him, sprang into the aisle and out the door and down the street, as if for his hunted life. Soon he realized that he was running alone. Therefore, he turned back and found all quiet. He then took his seat beside the bride-to-be and said, "Excuse me." She did. She hasn't spoken to him since. But the cry of "Fire!" did not make him a coward. It only revealed the cowardice that was already there.

These two men Abraham and Lot, must part company. They are stockmen. Their large flocks and herds make it necessary for them to take different directions. I can imagine they are standing upon the summit of a hill that gives a lookout over the surrounding country. Abraham generously gives Lot first choice. With an eye for the main chance Lot looks the situation over.

To the right is a wild, rugged country where the herdsman can find sustenance for his flocks if he is diligent. To the left is a marvelously beautiful country. The author of Genesis declares that it looked like "the garden of the Lord." As Lot gazes over that lovely country, he smiles his appreciation. "What a country!" he exclaims. "If I go in that direction, I can make a pile of money." But even as he looks, the smile changes into a frown.

"What is the matter, Lot?" I ask.

"That is a lovely country," he answers. "But look. Yonder are two cities, Sodom and Gomorrah. I have been on their streets. I have been disgusted by their loathsome wickedness. I am afraid of them for myself. I am afraid of them for my family." For remember that Lot is called a righteous man. As he looks in the other direction, he says to himself, "If I should choose that, I would not make as much money, perhaps, but I would have a better chance at the values that last. Such a choice would also give a better chance to those I love."

As he thus faced the appeal of getting on rapidly with greater moral risk and that of smaller material returns with less moral danger, which way did he go? We read, "Lot chose for himself." That is, Lot made his choice without any regard to the will of God. He made it asking only, "Where do I come in and what do I get out of it?" Of course, it was not his intention utterly to repudiate the will of God. He was only going to ignore God's will or, at best, to put it in second place. He still believed himself a religious man, but he was not allowing his religion to come first. Thus, as we see him making his choice with his eyes fixed on his own material interests, we are not surprised that he "moved his tent as far as Sodom."

Had I asked Lot the reason for his choice, he would doubtless have given one that sounded quite intelligent. "Business is business," he might have said. That is a revealing word. It is ever a danger signal. Whenever I hear a man use it, I am fairly sure that he has just beaten somebody out of something or is preparing to make an effort to do so. His reasons would have been quite as sane and modern as our own.

One Saturday morning years ago, I stood in front of the First National Bank in a certain town and talked to the president of that bank, who chanced to be the superintendent of my church school. There is an instinct of confession in all of us. If we have done something wrong, we do not feel quite so guilty if we confess that wrong to another. If we are preparing to do something wrong, we feel that we lessen our guilt by confessing ahead of time. So my friend said to me, "Preacher, I won't be with you tomorrow." Then he told me of certain plans that he had determined to carry out on God's holy day. When he had finished, I said never a word.

"You don't see anything wrong in that, do you?" he asked, with a touch of impatience.

"Do you?" I replied.

"Do you?" he also replied.

"Do you?" I still persisted.

Then, at last, honest man that he was, he said, "Well,

I suppose that is not exactly what a practicing Christian ought to do, but you preachers don't understand. A man must live."

"A man must live." When he said that, I knew he was headed in the wrong direction. When centuries ago they laid a cross on the shoulders of the choicest of all young men, naturally he shrugged it off saying, "A man must live." Thus we lost Calvary. No. He said and did the opposite. Himself he could not save. Nor can you and I. To seek to save life is to lose it, not in some far off yonder, but in the here and now. "Unless a grain of wheat falls into the earth and dies, it remains alone."

While Abraham chose within the will of God and remained in the hill country, Lot shunted the will of God into second place and moved his tent toward Sodom. Since he was going in the direction of Sodom, we need not wonder that he arrived. So in the very next chapter we read that Lot "dwelt in Sodom." In the nineteenth chapter we read, "Lot was sitting in the gate of Sodom." Not only had he reached Sodom, but, as another has suggested, he became mayor. I dare say I could get out his campaign literature. They wanted a business administration. Thus he is getting on famously, while Abraham among the hills is not by any means a pauper himself.

IV

Now, how do these two choices work out?

I am going to pretend that I am a reporter for some cosmopolitan daily and slip in and interview these two men. I go first to the office of Mayor Lot. Having been admitted, I ask a few questions. "Mayor, I understand that you have been living in Sodom now for twenty years. What have these years done to your religious life?"

I can see the care lines deepen in the mayor's face as he answers: "To be honest with you, Sodom has been vastly disappointing. A thousand times since I have been money-grubbing here, I would have gladly given all I have won to be under the oaks of Mamre with the sense of God I once had." [I am not reading something of my own into the story here. The New Testament states that Lot was "vexed in his righteous soul day after day" (II Peter 2:8).]

I go next into the hill country to see Abraham. "How are you getting on religiously?" I ask.

At that, his face glows like a sunrise. "I'm glad you asked me," he replied. "If you had not, I should have had to tell you anyway. The other day I had a visitor. I thought at first that he was just an ordinary angel, but I found that he was my Friend. When he came into my tent, the walls pushed back and the ceiling overarched. Since he has gone, he hasn't gone, for the place is sweet with his presence still."

I slip into the mayor's office for a second question. "Mayor, when you came into Sodom, did you find it a needy city? Did you find splendid lives going to waste? Did you find a community that was rotting down for lack of saving salt? Did you find desperate souls hungry for help?"

"Oh, yes," he answered, "there were many such."

"What did you do?" I continue. "You had a religious faith. Did you share it?"

"No," he says, "I really didn't have time." According to the story, if he had reached a man every two years, he might have saved the whole city. But he threw his chance away and went out at last, having exercised no more lift upon his community than the dead.

When I question Abraham as to what service he has rendered, he answers humbly, "God said to me that day 'I will bless you, and make your name great, so that you will be a blessing' " "You will be a blessing." That is the joy of living. Bishop Quayle used to say that it is the only vocation at which everybody can succeed. Little children can be a blessing. Youth in life's green spring can be a blessing. So it is with those in the stern stress of the middle passage. So it is even with those whose steps are hastening to where "the clouds are homing for the night."

Then this final question: "Lot, when you came to Sodom, you brought your family with you, didn't you?"

"Oh, yes," he answers. "What has Sodom done to your family?"

I can see the care lines grow yet deeper in his face as he answers. "I have lost them every one." When, aroused at last, he went to his sons-in-law and said, "God is going to destroy this city," they did not take him seriously. Instead, he seemed to them "to be jesting." He could no longer talk to his own about the things that matter most.

At my last visit to the tent of Abraham, I fail to find him. Instead, I meet his son Isaac. "You are the son of the family?" I question.

"Yes," he answers.

"Your father is not at home?"

"No, he is away today."

"Well, I suppose you will do. I am taking a religious census [I am sure they did that often in those days], and I want to ask this question. Is your father a religious man? Is he one of the saints?" Or, as we should say today, Is your father a Christian?

At that, Isaac laughs softly. Then he answers, "You don't live about here, do you?"

"No," I reply.

"I thought not. If you had lived in fifty miles of my daddy's tent, you would never have had to ask that question. Everybody knows where he stands. I was in a group of rough men the other day and someone mentioned his name. At once a kind of hush fell over them as one man said, 'I know him; he is God's friend.' "

I had a father like that. God could have said of him as he did of Abraham long ago, "I have chosen him, that he may charge his children and his household after him to keep the way of the Lord." It is only as we are fully committed that we can either find or give our best.

5

The Man Who Was a Convinced Crook

Your name shall no more be called Jacob, but Israel.
Gen. 32:28

Jacob is the younger of a pair of twins. When he first comes upon the scene, he is far less attractive than his brother Esau. In fact, he is not only unattractive; he is a bit repellent. He has so many qualities that we frankly do not like.

There are some people who lie with reluctance. There are others who lie with zestful glee. There are some who resort to dishonest measures under pressure because they seek a prize that they tell themselves they must have. There are others who resort to dishonest measures as a matter of choice. They not only enjoy the prize, but they enjoy the uplift to their ego that comes from outsharping their fellows. Jacob is of this second sort. He believes that a straight line is the shortest distance between two points only for stupid folks like his brother Esau. As for himself, a crooked line is the shortest distance to what he wants. He is quite sure that Esau will reap as he sows. But as for himself, he knows how to manipulate the laws of nature and to gather grapes of thorns and figs of thistles. Jacob is therefore what one might call a convinced crook.

Esau, the older brother, is rather attractive. He is a splendid animal. He is athletic. He has the healthy tan of summer suns upon his face. He has a body grown strong in matching his strength against the rugged wilds of the wide-open spaces. If he is quick to get angry, he is also quick to forgive. He is generous, generous even to his dotard and henpecked father, who has no appeal except the appeal of utter helplessness and weakness. Therefore we rather like Esau. Indeed, he would be popular in any generation. He would make a fine fullback. He could be the original for that song "For He's a Jolly Good Fellow."

But in spite of the ugliness of Jacob, and in spite of some fine qualities on the part of Esau, Jacob is the more promising of the two. It is true that he is selfish and scheming. It is true that he is as slippery as an eel; that he delights to live by his wits. Yet he does have some appreciation of the spiritual and the unseen. He values the privileges that have come to him as the heir of one who was a friend of God. Sad to say, his idea of God is quite unworthy. He rather looks upon him as one would look upon a wealthy and unloved relative whom he must please or run the risk of not being remembered in his will. He believes that God needs to be managed by just such a shrewd chap as he is. But at least he is taking God into account.

Esau, on the other hand, seems to have no sense of God at all. His fault is not so much that he is antagonistic to religion as that he has no interest in it. For him such values do not exist. The fact that he has been born in a great tradition, the fact that he is a part of that family through which all the nations of the earth are to be blessed, means nothing to him at all. He is interested in the chase. He is interested in his dinner, in his woman, in the sureness of his aim. But in the matters that pertain to religion he simply has no interest. This is not to say that Esau is a man of vicious purpose. He is rather a man of no presiding purpose at all. He is like a river without banks. There are no mighty compulsions in his life. There are no compelling "thou shalts," no compelling "thou shalt nots." Therefore, I repeat, Jacob is the more promising of the two. He does have some regard for those values that last.

This fact comes out in their first crisis. One day Esau came home from the chase with the natural hunger of a strong man who has spent the whole day in the open. As he passed Jacob's tent, he caught the aroma of dinner cooking. He therefore pulled back the flap of the tent and shouted, "Let me gulp down that red stuff."

It was just the chance for which cunning Jacob had been waiting. He now had Esau at a disadvantage and knew it. So he smiled winsomely and answered, "All right, brother, but before you eat, how about giving me that old birthright?"

At first Esau's eyes blazed with anger. Then he popped his fingers. "Take the thing," he answered. "I'm about to die. Then what good will the birthright do me?"

Here we see an example of the devil's skilled salesmanship. This cunning salesman does not keep his customers waiting. "Step into my establishment," he invites, "and right now get anything you want. I'll send you the bill later." The supreme power of temptation is that it offers its rewards immediately. That was Esau's undoing. He had to have his dinner at once. So we read that he sat down and "ate and drank, and rose and went his way." That was about all life meant to him. I can see him as he sits down to wolf his beans. Then, having emptied his dish, he rises, draws the sleeve of his goatskin coat across his greasy lips, and stalks away. "Thus Esau despised his birthright." Thus he despised the privilege of being the political and religious leader of his clan.

But Jacob set such a high price upon this birthright that he stole it. A little later, in a more shameful fashion, he also stole Esau's blessing. Then, having cheated Esau of both his birthright and his blessing, as his fellow gangsters would say today, Jacob "took it on the lam." He had to leave his father's tent. He never saw him again. He never saw his scheming mother again. From the tent of his father he made his way over to that of Uncle Laban. Since he was chased from home by his own wrongdoing, we might have hoped that in this new situation he would become a new man. But such was not the case. Nor was Uncle Laban any great help. He was a chip off the same block. He was himself a bit of a Shylock.

But when Jacob reached the tent of Laban, something did happen that gives us hope. The first person he met was Rachel. The story of their meeting has in it the radiance of romance and poetry. The music of their laughter is as winsome as the splashing of the water as it falls back into the well. We read that Jacob kissed Rachel and lifted up his voice and wept. A rather strange word. I have never quite understood that weeping. But of this we may be sure. Then and there Jacob fell in love with Rachel.

That gives us hope. Of course we know that anybody can fall in love. But what makes us hopeful is the fact that Jacob could remain in love across disappointing years. This indicates that among the much clay in his soul there was also some genuine gold. So deeply did he love Rachel that he agreed to serve seven years for her.

When at last the seven years were up, he married Rachel only to discover that Laban had wished off on him his weak-eyed older daughter, Leah. That same is a parable. Courting Rachel and marrying Leah is something that has happened over and over again. It has happened more often on the masculine side than on the feminine.

It is evident that in this first matching of wits the prize went to Laban. By such trickery Jacob was at once astonished and wounded. Listen to his outcry, "Why then have you deceived me?" How innocent and shocked he was! He seemed to say, "I did not know there was such a thing in the world as trickery, yet you have played it on me, your beloved kinsman." We are not to think that Jacob here was an utter hypocrite. He was horrified at the dishonesty of his Uncle Laban simply because it was not his own. It is amazing how very ugly sins that we justify in ourselves can appear when committed by the other fellow. Said a hefty sister the other day of one who was far more slender than herself, "I certainly hope I don't look like that." Even so, Jacob was honestly horrified to find that his uncle Laban had actually pulled a sharp deal on him.

But if Laban won the first round, the second went to Jacob. He made another deal with Laban, and the outcome was that, a few years later, Jacob, with both of Laban's daughters, with all his grandchildren, with the best of his flocks and herds, disappeared across the horizon. He made his way to the little brook, Jabbok, which he had crossed some twenty years before. At the time of that crossing he had had nothing but a staff in his hand and fear at his heels and a sob of loneliness in his throat. And now he was upon its banks again, ready to take possession of the land that was to be his. He had won and that by his own sharp wits.

I

Now it was upon the banks of this brook whose name signifies wrestling that an amazing miracle took place. It was here that Jacob found a new name and a new character. It is hard to believe. The whole story is astonishing. It takes us by surprise. Nobody expected any great change to take place in this man, least of all Jacob himself. This was true for a number of reasons. I mention only two:

1. Jacob was no longer young. He was now in the stern stress of the middle passage. He had reached that period where life tends to become most prosaic. He was now too far from the morning to be romantic and too far from the evening to be softened by the thought of going home. He had come to the point where the potatoes displace the pansies in the garden of life. Can a man be born anew when he is old? He can, but it is a rare miracle. Whatever vision splendid Jacob might have had, he had long since seen it fade into the light of common day.

Therefore we do not expect this slippery man, now in life's middle passage, ever to be greatly changed.

2. Jacob had made trickery pay. Thanks to his wrongdoing he was now a very successful man. Success in any enterprise is often a heady wine. Not everybody can take it. Many a man has grown intoxicated on himself to his undoing. But if success in general is too much for some, success in wrongdoing is the most dangerous of all. That made the case of Jacob one of extreme danger. After he had matched wits with all who crossed his path and had outsharped them all, why should he change? Sin is always dangerous, but it is never quite so disastrous as when it succeeds.

I think the greatest piece of fiction ever produced in America is *The Scarlet Letter*. There are two outstanding sinners in this story, Arthur Dimmesdale, the brilliant young Boston minister with a great reputation for holiness, and Hester Prynne, the young wife of an old man who at the time was thought lost at sea. These two shared in a guilty love. Hester was soon exposed. She gave birth to a child. Pearl, she called her, because she had bought her at a great price, her mother's supreme treasure. Then later she had to stand upon the pedestal of shame. She also had to wear exposed upon her breast a scarlet letter "A" signifying the fact that she was an adulteress. The author tells us that as she went down the street the little children often called the name at her. This hurt her especially because she knew that they did not know the meaning of the word. "It seemed to argue so wide a diffusion of her shame, that all nature knew of it; . . . the leaves of the trees whispered the dark story among themselves."

But nobody suspected the young minister. At least nobody except the wronged husband. Therefore, he went his accustomed way with the keen appreciation and approval of his people. But while he wore no scarlet letter outwardly upon his breast, he wore one inwardly upon his heart. For seven long years it made hell for him. At last one black night he flung out of bed, hurried down the streets of Boston to climb on the pedestal of shame where Hester had stood seven years before. Standing there, he uttered a wild wail that was echoed from house to house and was reverberated from the hills in the background; as if a company of devils, detecting so much misery and terror in it, had made a plaything of the sound, and were bandying it to and fro." Hester did not get away with her sin. For a long time Arthur Dimmesdale got away with his. But her suffering was as starlight to sunlight in comparison with that of the successful sinner. Jacob had for a long time made a success of wrongdoing. Yet even he was changed.

II

How did it come about?

God made the first move. That is always the case. In the old Genesis story when Adam sinned and lost his God, one would think that he would go up and down the aisles of Eden in search of him. Such was not the case. Instead, he went off and hid himself. It was God who had to make the first appeal. It was God who came calling to Adam as he does to you and me, saying, "Where are you?" We love him, if at all, because he first loved us. He is the Hound of heaven. He is the one who is constantly seeking us. He it is who even now is saying, "Behold, I stand at the door and knock." The first move toward our salvation is ever that of God.

The story is dressed in a queer garb, "A man wrestled with him." This wrestling God, this striving God, this seeking and wooing God is the supreme fact of revelation. It was to enable us to see and know him that Jesus came. He ever goes in quest of the sheep that is lost. By a thousand voices he calls to us. By every means that his infinite ingenuity can invent he wrestles with us. Of course, this was not the first time God had wrestled with Jacob. That had been a part of Jacob's daily experience. But here God got his chance and brought his wrestling to a climax.

The first reaction on the part of Jacob was resistance. If this had not been the case, there would have been no wrestling. It is impossible to wrestle with one who yields without resistance. Jacob resisted God. That is what he had been doing across the years. That is what all of us have been doing in some fashion. That is how many are changing the songful poetry of our holy religion into dull prose. Why are we not as strong and helpful as we could be? Why is not the beauty of the Lord resting upon us as the sunshine rests upon the hills? It is not because such beauty is for us impossible. It is, rather, because we have resisted God.

Yet God refuses to let us alone. That is the secret of our restless hearts. Why does not the sea lie down and be still? Why as if in pain is it always tossing? This is the answer. It is being played upon by two worlds. The heights are calling to it, but when it seeks to respond, the earth throws its muddy arms around it and says, "Stay with me." Yet though it stays with the earth, it can never forget the call of the heights. And man is that restless sea. He will always be restless until he finds his rest in the arms of God.

At last Jacob ceased to resist and began to cling. There came to him a revealing touch. To Jacob came a sense of his weakness, of his utter need. How it came I do not know. But he then not only ceased to resist, but he began to cry in desperation. "I will not let you go, unless you bless me." When Jacob said that, he was on the threshold of a new life.

But there was one step yet to be taken. So his seeming antagonist asked, "What is your name?" At that question I think Jacob blushed to the back of his bronzed neck. It is a question that in the language of the farm "plows close to the corn." What is your name, your character? What are you, seen through the eyes of your Lord? Jacob gave an honest answer. "Lord, you know my name. You know I am as slippery as an eel. You know I have lived by my wits. You know I have taken an unholy pride in trickery and cheating and lying. My name is Jacob, the Supplanter. Once I was proud of it, but now it fills me with shame."

Then what? In the West where I was preaching some years ago, an officer of the law one day put his hand on the shoulder of a man who had been living in that community for twenty-seven years. "What is your name?" he questioned. When the man gave his real name, the officer arrested him and took him back to his native state to stand trial. But when Jacob told his name, God did not punish him. He did not even rebuke him. Instead, he gave him a new name. This he did because it was true then as now, "If we confess our sins, he is faithful and just, and will forgive our sins and cleanse us from all unrighteousness."

Thus does this old story speak home to your need and mine. Though so old, it is as new as the sunrise. It is as new as the first smile that dimples the cheek of the mother's first baby. It is an experience every man needs, that every man may have. Who of us has not said,

> And ah for a man to arise in me,
> That the man I am may cease to be!

Who has not cried, articulately or inarticulately,

> I wish that there were some wonderful place
>   Called the Land of Beginning Again,
> Where all our mistakes and all our heartaches,
>   And all our poor selfish grief
> Could be dropped like a shabby old coat at the door,
>   And never be put on again.

There is such a place. That place is here and that time is now.

6

The Man Who Missed His Chance

> He did not do many mighty works there, because of their unbelief.
> *Matt. 13:58*

✣✣✣

Jesus was making a visit to his home town and to his home church. This was not the same visit as that recorded in the fourth chapter of the Gospel According to Luke. In the visit of which Luke tells us, there was perhaps more expectancy, more eagerness on the part of the villagers than in this. At that visit Jesus made a beautiful beginning. When he spoke in the synagogue, the congregation wondered at the words of grace that proceeded out of his mouth. As they listened, they said to themselves, "Everything that we have heard about him from other cities must be true."

Then Jesus spoiled it all. He made some remark about race relations. That was a touchy subject. He even hinted that the Jewish people were not the only people for whom God cared. That is something that we find it hard to tolerate even today. Not so long ago I knew a young minister of culture and of Christian grace who dared to tell his congregation that they were not the only ones who were going to enter the Kingdom. Almost immediately he had to resign. His people were so sure that they had a corner on God that they could no longer tolerate such preaching. Even so in his first visit, when Jesus implied that they themselves did not have a corner on the light, the worshipers broke up into a mob.

Now Jesus had come for another visit. In spite of their insults he could not leave them alone. In spite of their indifference he still cared. Therefore, he was coming back to give them another chance. He was quite sure that no failure need be final. When he proposed on another occasion to go back to Jerusalem, one disciple turned to him in amazement and said, "The Jews were but now seeking to stone you, and are you going there again?" But Jesus went because no insult can finally repel him. So here he was again in the city where he had spent his boyhood and where he used to work at the carpenter's trade.

The people were not entirely indifferent to him. They were astonished, even filled with wonder as to where he got his wisdom and his mighty works. But, in spite of their wonder, nothing came of it. I can imagine visiting Nazareth a week later. I meet a friend who is a typical member of the synagogue. "Simon," I say, "I hear that the Prophet visited you last week. I understand that he who has been making others glad by his mighty works has just come your way, that he was even now in your city. It must have been a high day. I suppose your community will never be the same. I suppose that you yourself will never be the same."

At that, Simon looks at me with an amazement that has in it a touch of contempt. "You are dead wrong," he answers. "I cannot see that the community is the least bit different. And speaking for myself, I certainly am not different. By this visit Jesus did nothing for me, nor did he do anything for anybody else so far as I can see. I believe that I did hear that he visited an old woman and healed her. I have also heard that he healed a child or two. But I do not take these reports very seriously. I rather think that these would have got well anyway."

Thus Simon missed his chance, a chance that might have produced in him a revolution so amazing that all life would have been forever different.

I

Now why did Simon and his fellow villagers miss their chance?

It was not because of circumstances. We do not read that it rained on this particular Sabbath that Jesus spent in Nazareth. Of course, had such been the case, that would have made any mighty works impossible. Nor was it the week during which there was a carnival or when one of the civic clubs was putting on its minstrel. That would have proved fatal. There seems nothing more sure than the willingness of the average member of the church to give way to any event of significance or insignificance that might come along. But Simon and his friends did not miss their chance because of circumstances.

No more did this Simon miss his chance because of any lack on the part of Jesus. Our Lord did really come to Nazareth. He was desperately in earnest in his coming. He was the furthest possible from being the type of character that he dreaded most—that is, the lukewarm, the halfhearted, the one who is never in earnest. Nobody takes seriously the man who is not in earnest. Listen to those on television, every one of whom affirms that his particular brand of cigarette is milder than any other. Even though we know that they cannot be telling the truth, they are halfway convincing. They tell their lies with such enthusiasm! Even a lie enthusiastically told will beat a truth, if that truth is told listlessly and without conviction.

Jesus did not fail for lack of earnestness.

No more did he fail because he was not able to live up to his extravagant promises. He was able to do for these Nazarenes, for this man Simon who ignored him, exceeding abundantly above all their power to ask or think. He is able still. He is "the same yesterday and today and for ever." At this moment he is able to do for us that which will change our drab and commonplace lives into lives that are full of beauty and power. So Simon and his friends did not miss their chance because of circumstances nor because of any lack on the part of Jesus.

Why, then, did Simon miss his chance? He missed it through his own fault. He missed it because he did not believe. He missed it for lack of faith. Now I know when I say that word "faith," we tend to grow listless. "Faith" is a Bible word that we have heard so many times that to many it is commonplace. Yet, as commonplace as it seems, it is that one something that opens the gates to a new life. It is also that something without which every door remains shut. Thus, it spells the difference between failure and victory.

II

Why is faith so important?

1. It is important because nothing constructive is possible without it. The writer to the Hebrews says, "Without faith it is impossible to please [God]." He might have left off the latter half of his sentence and have still spoken a truth of equal validity. "Without faith it is impossible." What? Everything is impossible. Without faith it is impossible to raise a crop. What could be more silly than walking over a newly plowed field and scattering golden grain with the knowledge that it would certainly rot in the ground? The raising of a crop of any kind is an act of faith.

Carrying on the daily business of life is a matter of faith. We cannot obey the laws of health without faith. Getting married is a matter of faith. It takes a lot of faith in some instances. It took faith for me to make such an adventure with only seventy-five dollars to see me through. Then think of the faith it took on the part of the bride who was going with me to a circuit so obscure that I simply could not get its location across to the newspaper man who had come to report our wedding. It takes faith to get married. It also takes faith to stay married. However great may be our mutual love, when faith fails, our marriage becomes a wreck.

It takes faith to make any kind of discovery. There may have been others in the days of Columbus who thought that the world might be round. But he was the only man who had faith enough to venture on his convictions. All the discoveries in the laboratory are made by men of faith. The man without faith simply says, "I doubt it," and does nothing. The man of faith believes enough to put his convictions to the test. Faith is important, then, because we can do nothing constructive without it.

2. Faith is important because, while nothing is possible without it, everything is possible with it. The man who made that assertion is called "the pioneer of faith." It was made by none other than Jesus Christ himself. He declared that faith as small as a mustard seed could juggle with mountains as a juggler might handle a ball. One day when he came upon his disciples after they had fumbled a great opportunity, he said to the father who had been disappointed by their failure: "All things are possible to him who believes." Jesus demonstrated that in his own life. None other ever showed as he that the victory that overcomes the world is the victory of faith. Everything is possible to him who believes.

Throughout the Bible as throughout history, over and over, the deciding factor between victory and defeat is faith. Here, for instance, are two groups who were approaching the same difficult crossing. One of them, the Egyptians, was cultured, well equipped, with every promise of success. The other was made up of men and women just out of slavery, ignorant, and, as seen through the human eye, with no chance of success. Yet it was the

Israelites that won, while the Egyptians failed. The difference, says the writer, was a matter of faith.

The power of faith in God is not surprising since faith is a source of power anywhere. The man who has faith in himself can do what he could not do without that faith. There is some truth in the statement, "We can because we think we can." I read somewhere of a gentleman who asked three men to undergo hypnosis. Having hypnotized them, he tested their strength on a gripping device. First he told them they were very, very weak. As a result they made an average of but 29. He then told them that they were very strong. They then averaged 141. That is, they were almost five times as strong when they thought they were strong as when they thought they were weak.

Faith in one of our fellows is a source of strength. I read somewhere that the soldiers of Napoleon used to call him "Old Two Hundred Thousand" because they reckoned that his personal presence was worth 200,000 ordinary men. The English just after Dunkirk might have called Churchill "Old Million," or even more, because he rallied them as none other could. He put heart and faith into them when heart and faith had run low. Faith, even in oneself or in one's fellows, is the source of power. It is not surprising, therefore, that vital faith in God is a source of limitless power.

III

Now, what is this power that lays hold of the very might of God?

Faith is more than an assent. It is not enough simply to say "I believe" and do nothing about it. A Gallup poll indicates that almost 99 per cent of the American people believe in the reality of God. But that faith is not transforming in a great many of their lives. It is merely an intellectual assent.

What is it to believe? To believe genuinely is to act. When I really believe, I go into action. Not only so, but I act in co-operation with God. Every movement toward man's salvation, whether in the realm of the physical or of the spiritual, is a co-operative movement. Faith that is real goes into action in co-operation with God.

For instance, one day Jesus came face to face with a man with a withered hand. He said to that man, "Stretch out your hand." That was exactly the impossible for this man. It was his big handicap, the thing that he could not do. Yet when, in faith, he undertook it, the impossible became possible. Again, our Lord confronted a man who had lain flat on his back for thirty-eight years. To this hopeless wreck he gave the command: "Rise, take up your pallet, and walk." Even while the man was telling how impossible it was for him to obey, having faith enough to make an effort, he actually did get up and walk. Faith co-operates.

It is the same in our personal salvation. What is it to be saved? For instance, take this promise: "If we confess our sins, he is faithful and just, and will forgive our sins and cleanse us from all unrighteousness." Suppose one comes confessing his sins. All he then has to do is to claim what Jesus has promised. When we do our part, we can count on him to do his. It is simply taking Jesus at his word, just as that nobleman did who came on behalf of his sick son. When our Lord said, "Go; your son will live," he did not keep tugging at the Master asking for some guarantee. On the contrary, we read, "The man believed the word that Jesus spoke to him and went his way." Personal salvation begins when we take God at his word and go our way to walk with him in newness of life.

The same kind of faith fits and undergirds us for the work of the kingdom. We have this definite promise, "Go . . . and lo, I am with you always." Here is another upon which I think I lean more and more as I get deeper into the years:

> So shall my word be that goes forth from my mouth;
> it shall not return to me empty.

It is our business to speak that word. It is our business to obey, to comply with the conditions and to leave the results with God. When we have gone as far as we can go, we can count on God to do his part.

What a wonderful illustration of this truth is given by that quartet who brought their friend to Jesus. Arrived at the place where the Master was teaching, they found the house so crowded that they could not even get close to the door. But they were so sure that if they would do their part Jesus would do his that they were dauntless. They therefore climbed to the roof, opened it, and let the man down at the feet of Jesus. Then having gone their limit, they looked down through the opening with full assurance that Jesus would not fail them. So what? He met their expectations. Their friend was healed.

What are we doing to bring our friends to Jesus for healing? What part do we take in gathering them into the fellowship of his Church? Let no one make excuse that he lacks knowledge or a golden tongue. There are three things that every one of us, regardless of his gifts, can do and get guaranteed results.

First, we can attend church ourselves. That is of vast importance. We need to remember that at Pentecost the Holy Spirit was poured upon individuals who were assembled for worship. The coming together of the people of God is still a matter of fundamental importance. We are not to neglect the assembling of ourselves together. Every man who attends church helps every other man to attend. Every man who stays away makes it easier for every other to stay away. He thus weakens his fellows, weakens his church, and hinders his Lord.

Then, we can invite others. Everybody who is willing can do that. Everybody! Since we can, we ought. This is a matter of primary importance. As we read the New Testament, we see that almost all those who came to Jesus were invited by somebody else. That has been true across the years. I dare say it is true of almost every one of us today. We came because we had not only a divine but also a human invitation.

A third something that everybody can do is pray. Now prayer is the mightiest power in the world. Prayer makes God real to the man who prays. Prayer also releases the power of God upon a given situation or upon a given individual. But prayer to be effective must be co-operative. It is not a substitute for action. It is not something we can do to relieve ourselves of tasks that we are too indifferent or too cowardly to perform. But when we go our whole length with prayer and effort, then we can count on God to work with us.

Archibald Rutledge, poet laureate of South Carolina, tells this story. He had two neighbors. One was an ex-convict who had spent many years in the penitentiary for the crime of murder. The other was a princely gentleman who owned an estate of five thousand acres. This estate abounded in game, quail, wild turkey, and deer. The owner so prized this wild life that he neither hunted himself nor allowed such privilege to anyone else. But the ex-convict seemed to delight in destroying the game, out of sheer spite, even shooting the turkey hens and the does. One day this wealthy neighbor came upon him as he was going home with his kill upon his back. When he tried to talk to him, the man only swore at him.

At last the harassed and perplexed man took his problem to Mr. Rutledge. "I have done everything I know to get on with this poacher. What have you to suggest?"

In answer the poet gave this wise and old-fashioned advice. "Why don't you plead with God to give him a change of heart. They tell me that love is stronger than hate."

It so happened that the friend took the advice seriously. Not only did he pray, but he went to see the man for whom he was praying. This he did in spite of the fact that he knew that his visit might have a distinct element of personal danger. But the poacher greeted him in friendly fashion. Not only so, but as he was leaving, this ex-convict said with backwoods shyness: "I am sorry for the trouble I have been to you. God came to me last night and told me to quit. From now on I aim to do so."

Even so, as we co-operate with God, the impossible will again and again become possible.

7

The Man Who Homed in the Heights

He makes my feet like hinds' feet, he makes me tread upon my high places.
Hab. 3:19

Here is a man who has won his way to the heights. He has climbed to where the air is pure and where he can have a vision of far distances. Not only so, but he moves upon these lofty places with the sure-footedness of a deer. One mark of old age, according to the preacher in Ecclesiastes, is this, "They are afraid . . . of what is high." But no such fear dogs the steps of this firm-footed prophet. It seems, therefore, that he is possessed of an immortal youthfulness over which the years have no power. He is as sure-footed as a deer.

But the deer is not only sure of foot; he is also fleet. The prophet is therefore not offering himself as a patron saint of the standpatters. He is not claiming merely to hold his own. Mrs. Lot has never moved one inch toward Sodom since leaving that doomed city, but this achievement is blacked out by the grim fact that she has never moved a single step toward the heights. This man, though he has climbed high, is still climbing. He is at once as nimble and sure-footed as a deer.

I

How did he win this victory?

It was not a mere matter of temperament. He does not give the impression of being by nature an optimist. No more was it born of circumstances. He had fought his way to this achievement at great cost.

He was evidently a man who had a keen eye. He saw clearly the grim evils both of his own nation and of the outside world. By these evils he was deeply perplexed. Through the history of his own people, especially through the great prophets, he had come to believe in a God of justice. The God of his faith was a holy God with eyes that were too pure to look upon iniquity. Yet iniquity was so prevalent, so universal, that he found it impossible to square his faith with what he saw. It certainly looked to him

> As if some lesser god had made the world,
> But had not force to shape it as he would.

His own nation, though claiming to be the chosen of the Lord, seemed to be more like the chosen of the devil. Injustice was everywhere. Violence stalked abroad unrestrained and unpunished.

If the situation at home was bad, the international scene was still worse. He saw that one nation, perhaps Assyria, was little more than a blustering, bloody bully. It was as ruthless as a beast of prey. It was as powerful as it was ruthless. Therefore it was winning one easy victory after another. The little nations were being caught in its net like silly, helpless fish. Those handling the net had grown arrogant and drunk on their own self-importance. Right seemed completely at the mercy of might.

Not only was this prophet a man with a seeing eye, but he was possessed of a sensitive heart. He could not but suffer in the sufferings of others. He felt like a man walking over a battlefield after the battle with the groans of the wounded in his ears. Suffering thus, he had to do something to help. Being neither soldier nor statesman, he felt that there was little that he could do. But there was at least one door of opportunity open to him. That was the door of prayer. "You also must help . . . by prayer." Paul wrote centuries later. The apostle was sure that those nameless saints to whom he was writing could, by their prayers, gird him with new strength and anoint his lips with grace and power. Even so, this prophet believed that he could help by prayer.

Acting on this faith, he turned eagerly and expectantly to God. But after he prayed, nothing at all seemed to come of it. Violence and corruption still stalked abroad. Helpless nations were still being caught in the net of the tyrant. Brutality continued on its bloody way unhindered. At last the heart of the prophet became so hot and desperate that he turned upon God with a frankness that seems quite shocking,

> O Lord, how long shall I cry for help,
>   and thou wilt not hear?
> Or cry to thee "Violence!"
>   and thou wilt not save?

"I am doing my best," he seems to say, "but you are doing nothing at all."

This harsh charge is born of his grief, to which has been added a touch of indignation. It is hard for a sensitive soul to look upon needless suffering without both pain and rage. I knew a Christian father years ago whose son became painfully ill. He sent for the one physician of the community. But it so happened that for some reason the physician had taken offense at this father, so he refused to come. In spite of this neglect the boy recovered. But recovery was not so easy for the father. He confided to a friend in the after days that he made up his mind that if his son should die he was going to take the life of the physician. Wrong? Certainly, yet understandable.

But here we see more clearly the greatness of this perplexed and half-angry prophet. In spite of the fact that God seemed to give no heed to his prayers, he refused to quit. Even when his head could not go along, his heart still clung to faith. "Being the kind of God you are," he seems to say, "you must give some answer. Therefore I am going to keep my place upon my watchtower with my faced turned toward the east. Thus, when the sunrise comes, I shall be sure to see it. But even if it never comes, I am still going to stay at my post."

II

What came of such bold and persistent prayer?

God answered. He always does. This is not to say that his answer is always yes. When Paul hurried into his presence, so sure that he would remove his thorn, he received an answer; but that answer was no. When Jesus, hoping that there might be some way of escape from his cross, prayed, "If it be possible, let this cup pass from me," God answered. But again his answer was no. Yet to real prayer God always gives an answer.

Not only did he answer this prophet, but his answer was not a denial of the grim situation about which Habakkuk complained. God made no effort to gloss things over. He did not seek to cover up rottenness with lovely words. He did not even say,

> God's in his heaven:
> All's right with the world.

He did not deny that the situation both within and without Israel was perilously grim.

No more did the Lord rebuke the prophet for his brutal frankness. In his presence we can say what we really think instead of saying what we think we ought to think. What a shocking prayer was that of John the Baptist. Though he prayed it through others, it was his very own. This John, sent of God to prepare the way of the Lord, was now at the end of his journey. Here he turned to Jesus and said, "I am disappointed in you; I am afraid that my ministry has been no more than a mistake. Am I right or wrong? 'Are you he who is to come, or shall we look for another?' " Insulting? Yet Jesus was not insulted. Instead, he gave that prayer a satisfying answer. Not only so, but when the messengers had gone, he proceeded to tell the people what a heroic soul John was. We can be frank, as Habakkuk discovered, in our prayers.

But if God neither denied the ugliness of the situation nor rebuked his prophet, he did deny his indifference and idleness. On the highway the other day I saw this sign, "Men Working." In answer to his prayer Habakkuk saw a vastly more impressive sign, "God Working."

> I am doing a work in your days
> that you would not believe.

God is the eternal worker. Jesus told us as much, "My Father is working still, and I am working."

That is a sure word for us today. God has not abandoned, and never will abandon, his world. He is working in our international situation. His victory may not be vastly impressive, but at least he has accomplished this. War has been stripped of its glamour. More people are now yearning and praying for peace than in any other day in human history. God is working among the nations.

He is working in his Church. There are times when his work there is disappointing. A certain Roman emperor once erected a triumphal arch in token of the fact that the last Christian had been swept off the earth, that the Church had been utterly destroyed. That triumphal arch has been so deeply trodden into the dust that history has forgotten where it stood. But the Church, in spite of all its failures, is still alive. In fact, it is today the one worldwide institution on this planet. This can be accounted for only by the fact that God is at work within his Church.

He is also constantly at work within the individual. Before your mother's lips kissed you, God was there. Through all your faltering days he has followed you. "Behold, I stand at the door and knock" is a constant experience. When the woman at the well desired to put off her decision until the coming of the Messiah, Jesus said, "I who speak to you am he." He is the one who even now is speaking to us, calling us from our restlessness to his rest, from our weakness to his power. God is the eternal worker.

III

Then God gave Habakkuk a glimpse of the end to which he works and also something of his method.

To what end is God working?

According to Mark Antony,

> The evil that men do lives after them,
> The good is oft interred with their bones.

Habakkuk believed the opposite. His affirmation of that conviction is the very heart of his message:

> Behold, he whose soul is not upright in him shall fail,
> but the righteous shall live by his faith.

That is, God is working toward the destruction of evil. The man whose soul is crooked is headed toward tragic failure, not in some distant eternity, but in this present world.

But while every evil thing is doomed, "the righteous shall live by his faith." That was destined to become one of the great words of the New Testament. Paul laid hold of it and made it his hope and his song. This word also is the rock upon which Martin Luther stood to preach his gospel that brought the Reformation. These great thinkers emphasized faith. They rejoiced that "the righteous shall live by his faith."

But for Habakkuk, I think, the emphatic word is "live." "The righteous shall live." While every evil thing is headed to destruction, righteousness, goodness can never be destroyed. The good man has a quality of life over which not even death has any power. "The light shines in the darkness, and the darkness has not overcome it." That is a fact of history. That is an experience of today that gives us a sure word for tomorrow. "The world passes away, and the lust of it; but he who does the will of God abides for ever."

God also gave Habakkuk a glimpse of what he was doing to destroy evil and to bring in righteousness. Since God is a king and not a despot, he permits his people to make their own choices. But when they make wrong choices, he sees to it that they do not get away with those choices. He was punishing them through the despotic power of Assyria. The prophet borrows this conviction from Isaiah. Here God speaks to this despotic power in these words,

> Ah, Assyria, the rod of my anger,
> the staff of my fury!

It is a historic fact that out of this punishment that finally ended in exile, Israel came to her richest experience.

"But how can a good God use such means?" Habakkuk questioned. "Though we deserve punishment, the one through whom we are being punished deserves it even more." Then God enabled him to see that Assyria was not going to escape. Instead, that bloody nation was doomed to die of its own conquests. The plunderer was going to be plundered, the destroyer destroyed. In the light of history we ought to see even more clearly than Habakkuk that for a nation to be despotic is to commit suicide. In every age hate begets hate and violence begets violence.

Here, then, is God's abiding word to this prophet,

> He whose soul is not upright in him shall fail,
> but the righteous shall live.

It may be hard to believe that the meek are going to inherit the earth. But it is still harder to believe that the nonmeek are going to get it. A man who has spent his life as a professional big-game hunter in Africa makes this assertion concerning the king of beasts: "No lion ever dies a natural death." But God can give himself to the nation or the individual that walks the way he himself is going. Hence, we may be sure with this prophet that "the righteous shall live."

IV

When he had fought his way to this high faith, what did it do for him?

1. It gave him a strength that would otherwise have been impossible. "God, the Lord, is my strength." The man of faith is the man of power. This is true because

faith opens the door for the incoming of God. Some of us can join with Isaiah in affirming,

> They who wait for the Lord
> shall renew their strength.

2. Having fixed his faith on God, he became independent of circumstances. When Jesus spoke to the Samaritan woman, he told her that she might find a well within. A well that would spring up to everlasting life. Thank God for those inner resources that enable us to carry on when outward resources are cut off.

3. This faith changed his sobs into songs. He came to an assurance without which we never arrive, but with which we can never miss the best.

Not so long ago I was a guest in a home of vast wealth. My host was said to be worth sixty million dollars. Of course I do not know how much that is. He showed me over his palace. He then took me riding in his wonderful car. But when on our return I was assisting my hostess from the car, she gripped my hands with a kind of frantic desperation and burst into tears. I went away with the conviction that though she had won so much she had somehow missed the one thing needful.

Here is the other side. In Texas years ago, when that state was putting on a drought in the superlative way that it does everything, I met an intimate friend, a man of deep consecration, who was a tenant farmer.

"How is your crop?" I asked rather stupidly.

He answered with a boyish grin, "I am not going to

make a thing. I have just come from looking over my crop, and I won't make a handful of cotton."

"I am so sorry," I answered with a sincerity that was all the greater because I was sure that this crop was for him not a luxury but a necessity.

In reply he answered even more cheerfully, "You know what I said as I looked at that parched and useless crop? I said, 'Lord, I thought you were going to take care of me this year through this cotton. Evidently you have some other plan.' "

At that he might have joined Habakkuk in singing this duet:

> Though the fig tree do not blossom
>   nor fruit be on the vines,
> the produce of the olive fail
>   and the fields yield no food,
> the flock be cut off from the fold
>   and there be no herd in the stalls,
> yet I will rejoice in the Lord,
>   I will joy in the God of my salvation.
> God, the Lord, is my strength;
>   he makes my feet like hinds' feet,
>   he makes me tread upon my high places.

His was a hard won faith, but it was beyond price.

8

The Man Who Experienced Easter

They recognized him.
Luke 24:31

"They recognized him." Thus it stands written of Cleopas and his companion. Who his companion was, we are not told. Since they journeyed to the same village, since they stopped at the same house, since one of them is nameless, the nameless one was in all probability a woman, the wife of Cleopas. We need to bear in mind that women in that day did not count. When Jesus fed the multitudes, we are told how many men were present. Each time there were so many thousands, "besides women and children." These were not numbered simply because they did not count.

But, be that as it may, this man of the long ago saw and recognized our risen Lord. Thus he came to an assurance without which there can be no real Easter. It is true that we might celebrate a date in the almanac with pomp and pageantry, but it would be no more than a date without this central certainty that was the priceless privilege of Cleopas and his companion. They came to know Easter, not simply as a date, but as an experience. The same transforming knowledge, I take it, is within reach of you and me.

This amazing story is really a gripping drama in four scenes.

I

As the curtain rises, we see two people, Cleopas and his companion, walking a stretch of road that leads from Jerusalem toward Emmaus. They are on their way home. Their journey, therefore, ought to be one of joy. There ought to be a spring in their step and a light in their face. Generally, to go home is a great privilege. It is hard to find one

> Whose heart hath ne'er within him burn'd
> As home his footsteps he has turn'd.

After all these years it is an experience to me that has never ceased to thrill. In truth it seems that it becomes more joyous as I get deeper into life and come more to appreciate the fine values that we find at home.

But for these there is no joy. They walk with lagging steps. They walk with tear-wet faces. This is the case because they are going home from a grave. That grave is very new. Theirs is, therefore, an experience that we have all had. That road has been hardened by the tramping of a billion feet. Its dust has been wet by countless tears. They are going back to take up the heavy burden of life without one whose presence has been their supreme joy. It is an old story, terribly unique for the one who is experiencing it, yet at the same time universal.

But there is something still more terrible and tragic in

their plight. The grave from which they are turning is unique. It is the grave not simply of one deeply loved but of one on whom they had centered their hopes for time and eternity. Therefore they say with sorrow unspeakable, "We had hoped that he was the one to redeem Israel." Thus they turn their backs on the grave of the one whom they counted on to assure a morning's joy with those we love, beyond this world with its griefs and its graves. They are going home from the tomb of their Lord. That is "sorrow's crown of sorrow."

II

When the curtain rises on the second scene, we see these same two, Cleopas and his companion, walking a different stretch of the same road. But this time they are not alone. Instead of being only two, they are three. That, too, is at once unique and universal. We are never alone. There is always one who is closer than breathing and nearer than hands and feet.

Here is John G. Paton burying his wife and baby at midnight in the far-off New Hebrides. He has selected this black hour to save their bodies from the cannibals. He tells us, "I must needs have gone mad by that lonely grave but for the presence of Jesus Christ."

Here is another man, Ernest Shackleton. He is speaking to a scientific society in London regarding his experiences in the Antarctic. He tells of his long and perilous trek over the ice and snow of that frozen country. "There were three of us," he declares. Then he adds with a boldness that almost seems shocking, "There were more than three of us.

We all felt that there were four." That sounds very like the counting of Nebuchadnezzar after he had cast only three men into the fiery furnace. When he opened the furnace door and counted again, there were more than three. There was a fourth. That fourth is always present—though, sad to say, like these two of the long ago, we often fail to recognize him.

As to why these failed to recognize Jesus, we are not definitely told. One reason, I think, was because he appeared in his resurrection body. This resurrection body was a spiritual body. Paul tells us, "It is sown a physical body, it is raised a spiritual body." The King James Version says, "It is sown a natural body; it is raised a spiritual body." But we are to understand that the spiritual is just as natural as the physical. The body of Jesus underwent such a change through his rising that some of those who saw him did not at first recognize him. The Bible is all the more convincing to me because of its frankness. Though these two knew Jesus well, they did not at once recognize him in his resurrection body.

But I think the supreme reason for their failure to recognize our Lord was that they had not the slightest expectation of seeing him. Their eyes were so fixed upon that tomb in the garden with its huge boulder and its red Roman seal that they could think of nothing else. That Roman seal represented the final effort on the part of Pilate to make the tomb secure as the Jewish authorities had requested. His effort was so puny that it almost has a touch of humor. It was as if some petty magistrate were to say to a policeman, "I do not want the sun to rise tomorrow. See that the gates of the morning are kept closed." Even that would be infinitely easier than keeping the Son of God locked within a tomb. Yet their gaze was so fixed upon this tomb that they were without any expectation of seeing their risen Lord.

"But," you say, "did not Jesus foretell his resurrection?" He certainly did. He also foretold his death. But, in spite of repeated warnings, his death took his disciples utterly by surprise. It shattered them as completely as if they had never heard of it. Even so, though he has told these of his resurrection, though he is even now walking beside them, their total lack of any expectation of his rising has so blinded their eyes that in spite of their burning hearts they fail to recognize him.

But the winsome Stranger begins at once to lead them toward certainty. With beautiful skill he induces them to tell their story. He knows that it will do them good to "unpack their hearts with words." So they tell him about their wonderful prophet, how mighty he was both in word and deed. They tell how the authorities condemned him to death and crucified him, how they thus put a black and bloody period to all their dear hopes and dreams. For they are quite sure that a crucified Christ can never do anything to redeem the world, can do nothing for themselves or for anyone else.

Then Jesus, with his wistful tenderness and compassion, says, "Oh, how foolish you are and how slow of heart to believe all that the prophets have said. The fact that your wonderful Lord was done to death on the cross is not a proof of his defeat; it is, rather, a sure pledge of his victory. He could have won in no other way. Was it not necessary that Christ should suffer these things and enter into his glory?" While he is thus explaining, these two, with a gasp of amazement, find that they are at the steps of their own front door.

Not only are they amazed, but I think they are filled with regret. They are afraid that their unknown companion will go. This simply will not do. Therefore, they turn to him and all but lay violent hands on him as they say, "Stay with us, for it is toward evening and the day is now far spent."

"They constrained him," says the text. We all know how to invite a friend whose presence we really desire. We also know how to invite when we wish to save both our manners and our dinner. All we have to do is say, "You won't go to dinner with me, will you?" Anybody knows that the only sensible answer to that is "No." But they "constrained" Jesus. "So he went in to stay with them." Then as now, he never fails to accept when he is really invited.

III

The third scene takes place within this humble little home. Host and hostess assemble with their guest about the table for the evening meal. It seems to have been quite frugal. At least, only bread is mentioned. But thus assembled, they ask their guest to give thanks. When he complied with their request, there is that in the way he speaks to his Father and that in the way he breaks the bread and gives it to them that calls forth old memories and brings to resurrection dead hopes. Then it happens: they know in the deeps of their souls that this amazing guest is their risen Lord. "Their eyes were opened and they recognized him."

No sooner have they recognized him than he vanishes out of their sight. That may seem a bit disappointing. It may seem like bringing this part of the story to an anticlimax. But it is not an anticlimax; it is the opposite. You will remember that there were three periods in the ministry of Jesus. First, there was the period when he was with us in the flesh, when he spoke through human lips, when he ministered through human hands, when he walked on human feet. Then, there was that brief period of forty days after his resurrection when he would appear and disappear. He would manifest himself to the physical senses and then vanish out of sight. What was the purpose of this? We are not told. But we can give a very intelligent guess. I think he was preparing his friends for the realization that he was no less near when unseen than when seen. He was preparing them for the days in which we live. Today we know him, not by sight, but by faith. Not as a visible Christ, but as one who is invisible.

This is not a loss, but a gain. I know there are some who think otherwise. These sometimes sing wistfully,

> I think when I read that sweet story of old,
> When Jesus was here among men,
> How He called little children as lambs to His fold,
> I should like to have been with them then.

But a greater privilege is ours. This is the testimony of Jesus himself. He said to his friends, "It is to your advantage that I go away." Why is this the case? By his going away, he has come the closer to us. Since he has gone away from our physical sight, he has come in the person and power of the Holy Spirit. Surely that is to our advantage. This is true because a spiritual Christ can do for us what a physical Christ could not do. A physical Christ is limited. If he is at one place, he cannot be at another. But a spiritual Christ can be with everybody, everywhere, every moment. It is this fact that made for the change of attitude on the part of these friends toward his going. Viewed in prospect, it filled them with bitter sorrow. But when they had followed him as far as Bethany and seen him ascend, "they returned to Jerusalem with great joy." We may be sure, therefore, that the vanishing of Jesus brought to these two not poverty but richer wealth.

IV

The fourth scene is one that continues unto this hour. When these two become certain of Jesus, when they are aware that the Christ whom they saw crucified is alive forevermore, they cannot sit still in their little cottage. Though they have warned their guest just a few moments ago not to travel in the night because they feel that night travel is a bit dangerous, they completely forget that warning. So we read "And they rose the same hour and returned to Jerusalem."

How tired they must have been! They had already

walked seven miles, then seven miles back. That made fourteen miles they had to walk, much of it in the night. It must have been a bit wearying. But they forgot all about their weariness. They had a story to tell that put wings upon their feet because it put a song in their hearts. On reaching Jerusalem, they shared their story with their fellow believers. They also listened to the story of how Jesus had appeared to Simon. It seems as if our Lord could hardly wait to get the door of his tomb open to manifest himself to this man who loved him so deeply and who had denied him so shamefully.

Now it was their experience of the risen Jesus that sent this little handful of believers to lift empires off their hinges and to remake the world. Without political power, without financial backing, without the training of the schools for most of them, they went about their task. What was their secret? It was this certainty, this awareness of the risen Lord. Armed by this, they went out on their mission that continues to this very hour. Not only so, but they went into a world more dead and disintegrated than ours and utterly remade it. This they were able to do because they knew Easter not simply as a date but as a vital, living, abiding experience.

This is the unspeakable privilege to which our Lord is calling us. I believe in the resurrection of Jesus for many reasons. I think as a historic fact it is one of the best proven in human history. There are so many evidences for the Resurrection, evidences that for me at least are unshakable. But the supreme evidence is to know Jesus himself as a personal Savior and friend. Such knowledge, at the same time, makes evidences in a sense unnecessary. Whatever evidences we may have, if we do not know him, we have failed to find the truth of the Resurrection. But however little we may know of evidences, if we know him, we have enough. It is well to know about bread, but no knowledge of bread can satisfy my hunger. It is well to know about water, but no knowledge of water can quench my thirst. It is well to know botany, but no book of botany can spill from its pages the perfume of a honeysuckle or the red of a rose. It is well to know astronomy, but no book of astronomy can light the east with a sunrise or can bejewel the sky with stars. It is well to know about Jesus, but nothing can take the place of this: "Their eyes were opened and they recognized him." To experience the risen Lord is the supreme evidence of the Resurrection. It is what changes Easter from a date into a radiant experience.

9

The Man Who Missed Something

What do I still lack?
Matt. 19:20

We of today are not greatly disturbed about our sins. Though we may confess that we are "heartily sorry," our confessions as a rule are not red with shame nor wet with tears. Sorry we may be, but too often we are not sorry enough to "amend our ways." Having cheaply confessed that we have gone in the wrong direction, we continue to travel the same disappointing road. Somehow it seems hard for us to believe that even God is greatly grieved over our very respectable and decent sins.

But if we are not disturbed by any deep sense of guilt, we are disturbed by gnawing hungers and burning thirsts. Though the day laborer now has luxuries of which no ancient monarch ever dreamed, we are still restless and dissatisfied. Few are ready to say to any magic moment "Stay, thou art so fair." We can even outwail Thackeray as he sobs, "Vanity of vanities, who of us gets his desire, or getting it is satisfied?" This might serve as the theme song for multitudes:

I do not know, I do not care
How far it is to anywhere;

I only know that where I'm not
Is always the alluring spot.

Therefore many of us find a spokesman in that charming gentleman who in the long ago came to Jesus with this question: "What do I still lack?"

I

What indeed? At first glance, nothing at all. He seems to have had everything. Of all those who came face to face with Jesus during the days of his flesh, none was more winsome, none seemingly more to be envied than this man. Who he was, we are not told. But the ages have agreed in giving him a name. It is one that fairly glitters. He is called the Rich Young Ruler.

He was rich. Of course we are aware that no amount of money can satisfy the deep longings of the heart. Yet wealth is not something to be despised. Money is power. It may be a source of vast good or of vast evil. It is dangerous only when we relate ourselves to it in a wrong way. As a master it is the very devil. As a servant it can work wonders. It is a kind of Aladdin's lamp by which we can summon endless helpers to do our bidding, from the feeding of the hungry and the clothing of the naked to the making of friends who will at last receive us into eternal habitations. This man, being rich, was therefore possessed of great power to do evil or to do good.

He was a ruler. This does not mean that he was governor of a state. It rather means that he was a member of the Jewish Sanhedrin. He was a part of the highest court of his day. As such he was a blueblood, an aristocrat. He was, in a sense, born to the purple. It is a great privilege to be wellborn. It is fine to have an excellent family tree. This is the case in spite of the fact that if we climb high enough up any family tree we are likely to find something hanging there that is not an apple. This young man, being wellborn, had for that reason added power either to hurt or to help.

He was young. He faced life with shoulders unbent by burden-bearing, with eyes undimmed either by years or by tears. He had a whole life to invest in the service of the highest.

> How beautiful is youth! how bright it gleams
> With its illusions, aspirations, dreams!
> Book of Beginnings, Story without End,
> Each maid a heroine, and each man a friend!

In thus emphasizing the importance of youth, I am not minimizing the importance of middle and of old age. There is a great deal of sentimental rot talked about youth, as if it were the only part of life worth living. That is emphatically not the case. I was on a train the other day when a young mother was trying hard to manage her obstreperous small boy who was disturbing everybody in the car. At last a sweet old lady broke in with this word: "Let him do as he pleases. Remember, he won't have any good time after he has grown up."

What utter nonsense! A sweet old man who was listening found it hard to keep from telling her how dead wrong she was. I think I had a normal youth and a normal middle life, but I am having a still better time now as I am coming toward the late afternoon. Hence I am inclined to agree with Bernard Shaw that youth is wasted on young people.

At any rate it is surely not the purpose of God that life should begin in a radiant climax and end in a drab anticlimax. Instead, here is his intention:

> The path of the righteous is like the light of dawn,
> which shines brighter and brighter until full day.

I therefore congratulate you who are young mainly because you have the best possible opportunity by your early dedication to God to guarantee that life for you will climb toward an ever-increasing climax. This door was open to our young ruler.

This young man was further possessed of a deep moral earnestness and courage. When he heard that Jesus was passing, he gathered his garments about him and ran to fall at his feet. People do not run often in that land of leisure. He ran when nobody else was running. He knelt when nobody else was kneeling. It does not take much courage to stampede with the crowd. But to run alone and to kneel alone, that takes courage of a high order.

His courage is further evident because of the wide social chasm that divided these two. This young ruler was a blue blood, a patrician. Jesus, at whose feet he was kneeling, was a peasant whose palms were calloused by handling the tools of a day laborer. Furthermore, all the class to which this ruler belonged had already turned thumbs down on Jesus. Hence he was alone in thus showing honor to this carpenter. He was a man of high moral earnestness and courage.

He was a religious man. Not only so, but he had taken his religion seriously. He had kept up his fences. When Jesus put to him the moral law, he was able to look into those clear eyes and say, "All these I have observed from my youth." Do not think he was not telling the truth. What he said was so true that the heart of Jesus went out to him with a deep love of approval. "And Jesus looking upon him loved him." Of course he loved him no better than he loves you and me, but he could love him with a love of approval such as he cannot give to some of us.

We may not be surprised that this young ruler had kept himself free from murder or from stealing, but he had also kept the seventh commandment, which is so often not taken seriously by youth in any age. Today there is even a certain type of psychiatrist that approves its breaking. Yet it is a fact that those who break it lessen their chances for marriage if they are girls. Further, they lessen their chances of making a go of marriage whether they are boys or girls. The tragedy of sacrificing upon the wayside altar is that so often when we come to the supreme sacramental moment of life, we have nothing to give.

Now it was this young man, rich, religious, clean, and lovable, who said, "I have missed something. What is it?" What did Jesus answer? He did not call him an introvert. He did not accuse him of being morbid. He did not send him away saying, "You have arrived." Instead, he said to him, "You lack one thing." Here, then, are two credible witnesses to the fact that he had missed something—Jesus and the man himself.

II

What did he lack?

It was not decency, uprightness, integrity. It was not earnestness and high courage. It was not reverence; he was still able to bend the knee. What, I repeat, had he missed? He himself rightly diagnosed his case. He had missed eternal life. He had missed the life that comes from knowing God through Christ. "This is eternal life, that they know thee the only true God, and Jesus Christ whom thou hast sent." Thus he had missed the one something that can satisfy in time and eternity.

A friend of mine, an unlettered minister of deep consecration, tells this story: He went one day to visit a brilliant and rather cruel agnostic who took delight in exposing the ignorance of certain ministers who came to his backwoods village. He found my friend an unusually promising prospect, so he led him at once into his spacious library. Here he handed him one heavy and forbidding volume after another, asking each time, "Brother, have you ever read that?"

"No," my friend answered modestly, "I didn't know there was such a book."

At last, when there was a moment of silence, the preacher said: "Now I have seen your books, I'd like to show you mine. I have a book here that I deeply love. If you wouldn't mind, I would like to read you a word from it." So he read,

> He was wounded for our transgressions,
>   he was bruised for our iniquities;
> upon him was the chastisement that made us whole,
>   and with his stripes we are healed.

Then the minister prayed. His prayer went something like this: "Lord, this is the smartest man I ever saw. He knows everything, it seems. That is, he knows everything except you. He don't know a thing about you, Lord. That's what breaks my heart." Then, says my friend in his quaint way, "he just fell on his face and got religion."

Even so, this young ruler had everything except God. But as he knelt at the feet of Jesus, his face one eager wistfulness, our Lord told him how he might find what he had missed.

III

What did he tell him?

His answer was drastic. At the close of one of my sermons a friend gave me this sharp criticism, "You tried to perform a major operation this morning without making an incision." Certainly that was not the case with Jesus in dealing with this eager seeker. He fairly laid the patient open with this word: "Go, sell what you possess and give to the poor, . . . and come, follow me." How drastic! He was to part with vast wealth, wealth not only of worth in itself but of high sentimental value since it had probably come to him touched by the fingers of his fathers.

There is that in this command that is unique. There is also that which is universal. The unique is the selling and the giving away. Of course our Lord does not ask that of every man. Why did he demand it of this young ruler? Because he saw what came first with him. He saw that, while he was eager for eternal life, he was yet more eager for things. He had great possessions, but his possessions also had him. He was a bit like a fly on a piece of Tanglefoot. The fly might say with emphasis, "My Tanglefoot." But, with yet greater emphasis, the Tanglefoot might answer, "My fly."

But what is universal in this command? It is this— "Follow me." That is the one essential. This young ruler might have complied with the first part of this command and still not have become a disciple. He might have sold everything, he might have given every penny away, and still have missed eternal life. "If I give away all I have, and if I deliver my body to be burned, but have not love, I gain nothing." What Jesus was after was not primarily the selling and the giving. What he was after was the young man himself. He was after obedience. That is Christianity, the whole of it. It is Christianity in its course and in its consummation. It is the least one can do and begin to be a disciple. It is the most he can do in time and in eternity.

IV

What response did this man make?

He did not rise to his feet with bewilderment looking

out from his once clear eyes. He did not say, "I came in all earnestness to learn the way of life, but you have merely perplexed me. I do not know what I ought to do." He did know. He knew as well as we know what we ought to do. What, I repeat, was his response? "He went away." That does not mean that Jesus put his hands on his two youthful shoulders and pushed him away. He did not have to go. But, though feeling deeply the appeal of Jesus, he of his own choice went away.

No wonder our Lord looked after him and said with an ache in his heart and a sob in his throat, "How hard it will be for those who have riches to enter the kingdom of God."

The disciples could hardly believe what they saw and heard. They turned on Jesus with a question that is a gasp of amazement. "Then who can be saved?" Who, indeed? That is always the big question. Who cannot? Well, in all sober sense, no one who refuses to meet the conditions, no man who turns away from him who is the life. Every step away from him is a step toward death.

Who, then, can be saved? Anybody who will meet the conditions, any man who will obey or even be willing to obey. Here is one who seems far more hopeless, far less promising than this young ruler. Matthew was also a lover of money. He loved it so deeply that he had sold his good name for it. He had sold his patriotism. He had sold his faith. But when he encountered Jesus, his sorry bargain began to break his heart. Then, one great hour, he looked up from his ledger to find himself face to face with our Lord. "Follow me," Jesus said to this renegade whom nobody wanted.

Then what? Did Matthew give all his wealth away? I do not know. Did he sob? Again I answer, "I do not know." Did he shout or sing or pray? My answer is still the same, "I do not know." But I do know this: he did the one essential thing. He did that which brought him newness of life. He "rose and followed him." Thus by his obedience he won what this winsome young man longed for, and might have had, but missed. Have you missed something? Is that something the knowledge of God through Christ? Then you can find it by walking the path of obedience.

10

The Man Who Despaired

So I . . . gave my heart up to despair.
Eccl. 2:20

The mood of despair is one that is quite prevalent in our day. The seat of the scornful may still have a few vacancies, but the seat of the mournful is filled to overflowing. When Clement Attlee was prime minister of Britain, Winston Churchill paid him this highly questionable compliment, "Mr. Attlee is a very modest man, with a great deal to be modest about." Even so, this Preacher who is little more than a walking wail seems half gleeful in his gloom, because he feels that he has so much to be gloomy about. But before we become proud of our despair, or even before we become complacent about it, I think it might be well to face certain facts.

I

1. Despair is not an asset but a liability. This is the case however well we may justify it. Despair is a kill-joy to its possessor. It takes the spring out of his step, the sparkle out of his eye, and the song out of his heart. It was even so for this cynic. He said frankly that he hated life. He declared that those who were dead were better

off than those who were alive, but that the most fortunate of all were those who had never been born. He found nothing either glad or beautiful in life. He said of laughter that it was mad. He never saw anything humorous, not even when he shaved.

Now, it is bad to be born blind. It is almost equally bad to be born without any sense of humor. Over the door of an old monk's cell in Scotland there are these words, "Sweeten bitter things with gentle laughter." That is something that is worthy of both careful and prayerful consideration. Blessed is the man who can laugh *with* others and who can laugh *at* himself. The man who has no sense of humor is almost sure to major on minors.

Furthermore, despair paralyzes all effort toward building a better world, a better nation, or a better individual. This cynic was a greatly gifted man. He had a tremendous capacity to help; but, in spite of that fact, he was far more harmful than helpful. This was the case because he was a convinced son of despair. For him life had neither purpose nor meaning. Men were mere beasts. All women were bad. There might be one good man in a thousand, but that seemed doubtful. Worse still, there was nothing anybody could do about it, since the crooked could never be made straight. His was a drab world where there was nothing new under the sun, least of all a new man. Hence his only recourse was to get drunk and forget the whole mess.

He reminds me of a story they tell in the mountains of a widow who sent her two sons across a swift, shallow brook to gather a wagonload of apples. As they came back, on the home side of the brook, they had to climb a steep embankment. The heavy pressure of the apples against the hind gate of the wagon bed pushed it out, and all the apples fell into the water. Jimmy, the younger son, went home to report. When his mother had heard the tragic story, she asked, "Where's John?" The son answered, "He's sittin' down on the bank of the creek, cussin'." It was even so with this very shrewd cynic.

Not only is the son of despair useless, but he is a positive menace. Courage is contagious, but so is cowardice. I am thinking of one of the greatest laymen I ever knew. He could be counted upon to be present at every service of his church when humanly possible. Not only so, but his coming was like turning on a new light. "Thank God!" I would say in my heart as he took his place in his pew. "I can preach better because of his presence." Then, perhaps, only a few feet behind him would come some son of despair, who would prompt me to say, "The Lord helping me, I will try to preach anyway." If, therefore, we have despaired, we are not only robbing ourselves but our fellows as well.

2. A second fact that we need to bear in mind is that if we are in despair, it is very likely our own fault. Of course, we do not believe this any more than did this ancient cynic. He believed that his despair was justified by his frank facing of facts. He had been everywhere and had seen everything. Not only so, but he had looked with far clearer eyes than those of his stupid fellows. Having thus looked and having found everything bad, he was half happy in reaching the conclusion that there was nothing to do but to give way to despair.

But, as a matter of fact, despair is not a child of circumstances. It is rather a child of the heart. If despair were really born of our circumstances, then all those who are experiencing the same dark circumstances would also experience the same degree of gloom. But that is not the case at all. We can verify that fact both in our own experiences, as well as in those of others.

There was, for instance, a company of men on board an ancient merchant vessel. That vessel had been battered by a storm for almost two weeks. It was threatening to fall apart at any moment. So desperate was the plight of those on board that Luke tells that all hope that they should be saved was taken away. But while despair had conquered the vast majority, its victory was not complete. There was one radiant and gallant-hearted exception. Paul could see the tragic circumstances of this vessel and of those on board just as clearly as anyone, yet he stood up in that atmosphere of despair and shouted this great word, "Take heart, men."

I am thinking of two women, both in trying circumstances, since both are invalids. One of them has become a petty tyrant. She is a dispenser of despair. The other, though a still greater sufferer, is yet unbelievably radiant. As I was visiting her, the nurse whispered to me, "She is in agony every waking moment." At that, her already bright face became brighter still. "You know," she said, "I catch myself wishing that I could bear the pain of others. I have learned so well how to handle it."

Naturally it is easier to despair in some circumstances than in others. Yet if despair were purely a child of circumstances, it would be easy to divide the hopeful from the hopeless. All we would have to do would be to find the poverty-stricken, the afflicted, the failures, the jalopy drivers, and over against them put the rich, the healthful, the successful, the drivers of Cadillacs, and say, "These sons of good fortune are always abounding in hope, while these sons of ill fortune are always in despair." But such would not be the case at all. It follows, therefore, that if we are in despair it is our own fault. This ancient preacher confesses as much. He declares, "I . . . gave my heart up to despair." He did not have to despair; he simply made a spineless surrender to despair.

3. A third fact that we should bear in mind is this: Since despair is so hurtful to ourselves and to others, it is more than a misfortune. It is a positive sin. No man has a right to steal my money. Even so, no man has a right to steal what is more priceless than gold—my courage, my expectancy, my hope. Yet even the best of us are too often guilty of this ugly and hurtful sin.

Some time ago I went to hear a friend preach. He is a man of unusual ability and genuine consecration. His theme was "The World Outlook." He discussed the situation with some intelligence and truth. But he offered not one ray of hope. The picture he painted was one of utter gloom. He left those who took him seriously without even a horizon where they might hope for a dawn. I felt then, and I feel still, that he preached a wicked sermon. It was not only unchristian; it was anti-Christian. Whenever we by any means take the heart out of our brother and send him bumping away on four flat tires, we have done a wicked and cruel thing.

I do not wonder, therefore, that wise and consecrated John Watson declared, as he came near the sunset of his life, "If I had my ministry to go over again, I would preach more comforting sermons."

> Comfort, comfort my people,
>   says your God.
> The Lord God has given me
>   the tongue of those who are taught,
> that I may know how to sustain with a word
>   him that is weary.

There are so many weary folks. Every Sunday they come to our churches with wistful hearts, praying that the minister may say something that will give them strength to climb the next hill. Much of the teachings of our Lord can be summed up in this word: "Take heart." To encourage is Christian; to discourage is wicked and anti-Christian.

II

Naturally, if we are to give courage to others, we must have courage in our hearts. We cannot give what we do not possess. We must be hopeful if we would inspire hope. To tell a despairing friend, "Take heart," when our own face is dark with gloom is to be downright exasperating. Still worse is that essence of stupidity. "Cheer up. You do not have to die but once." To die once is usually fatal. How, then, shall we help ourselves to attain a contagious courage?

Look well to your body. So far as in you lies, enjoy good health. Refuse to work to the point of exhaustion. Bear in mind that the most Christian thing that a tired person can do is to rest. Jesus taught us that, both by precept and by example. He said to his own, "Come away by yourselves to a lonely place, and rest a while." I think Jesus would have looked upon it as a positive sin to work himself to such a point of exhaustion that he was no longer able to serve at his best.

Elijah was a great man. But his greatness is not indicated by his attitude under the juniper tree. Here his lion-like voice dwindles into the poor squeak of a Mickey Mouse. He tells the Lord that he is the only good man in the world, and that he hopes that he will not be in the world much longer. In requesting for himself that he might die, he is less than sincere. Had he really desired death, his prayer would not have been necessary. All that would have been necessary would have been for him to stop over in Jezreel for an hour or two. Jezebel was prepared to answer his prayer before he ever prayed it. It is far harder for one to be hopeful if one is physically exhausted.

Then, remember that your situation is not entirely bad. The situation that this cynic faced was nothing like he pictured it. He declared that while there was order in the realm of the physical, there was chaos in the realm of the spiritual. Hence, he had seen fools on horseback while princes walked. He had seen the wicked reaping the reward of the righteous, while the righteous reaped the reward of the wicked. He believed that what a man sowed in his field he might reap, but what he sowed in his own moral life he would not reap. Yet this law of sowing and reaping is eternally true. It works all the time, and it works everywhere.

The trouble with this very keen man was that he had taken a superficial view. To the man who sees things clearly and who sees them whole, men do reap as they sow. Though a good man may suffer in purse and suffer in body, yet if he meets his calamity within the will of God, all things will work for his good. Therefore the picture painted by this cynic simply did not exist.

Certainly there is much that is bad in our world, but there is also much that is good. Jesus spoke of four kinds of soil. There was the wayside soil, useless because it was so hard. There was the rocky soil, also useless because it was shallow. There was the thorny soil, equally useless because it was overcrowded. But there was some good soil. There was soil so good that it brought forth thirty, sixty, and a hundredfold.

Now just as no situation is wholly bad, no more is any individual. We have a great love for painting scenes and persons absolutely white or absolutely black. But such a picture is always wrong. The very best of us could stand a little improving. That we all know. I have seen more than one minister who, by his lack of perfection, gave me a good argument for purgatory. Even so, there is something good in the worst of us. I have never really known one who was so bad that I did not find some little flower of decency growing in the fetid soil of his soul.

But the supreme antidote to despair is faith. Faith in God and faith in men. One of the pet horrors of our day is the superficial optimist. He can be a bit of a pest. Out of wishful thinking, he may sometimes see a fountain where there is really only a mirage. But he is surely no worse than the superficial pessimist. Yet we have a great tendency to rebuke the one and to praise the other. Just why this is the case, I do not pretend to know. Personally I have never been able to grow enthusiastic over one whose biggest virtue is that he can see nothing in the most delicious of doughnuts but the hole!

My friend who preached that depressing sermon would have told you with conviction that he was simply facing the facts. He was facing them in part, but the trouble was that he did not face all the facts. No man can face all the facts and be utterly cast down. No man can face all the facts and be a confirmed son of despair. The ten spies faced all the facts of their situation except one. That was the fact of God. The result of not facing that fact was that they became a burden to themselves and a menace to others.

Of all the books that face the facts in their grim ugliness, none surpasses the Bible. Yet it is the most hopeful of all books. It has kindled more courage in the hearts of people than any other book ever written. Why is this the case? It is the case because it is constantly facing the worst in the light of the fact of God. There are two words that it puts together again and again. They are these: "But God."

"We all once lived in the passions of our flesh . . . and

so we were by nature children of wrath. . . . But God . . . even when we were dead, . . . made us alive." That changes death into life.

"And the patriarchs, jealous of Joseph, sold him into Egypt." They could hardly have gone beyond that. His seemed a fate worse than death. That cruel deed should have been final. Such was the purpose of his brothers. As they dusted him off their hands, they were sure that he would end in the oblivion of a slave pen. "But God was with him." Thus the road they thought would end in oblivion ended in an immortality of usefulness.

Even though men knew nothing better to do with Jesus Christ than to nail him to a cross, that was not the final damning word. "But God raised him from the dead."

Thus, ever over against the blackest that men can be or do, stands the radiant fact of God. This is our salvation. For God and despair can never keep house in the same heart at the same time. Therefore let us join with Paul in this prayer, "May the God of hope fill you with all joy and peace in believing, so that by the power of the Holy Spirit you may abound in hope." This abounding hope will not only save us from despair but give us a priceless treasure to share with others.

11

The Man Who Lost His Temper

So he turned and went away
in a rage.
II Kings 5:12

Of all the books that "hold the mirror up to nature" none, I think, is quite equal to this book we call the Bible. Here is a story that is at once so human and so childish that we would laugh out loud were it not at the same time so tragic. A very prominent man comes to the prophet Elisha seeking a cure for a desperate illness. In response to his request the prophet gives him explicit directions for his healing. But those directions do not appeal to the patient. They rather prick his pride. Therefore in hot anger he walks out on his physician, forgetting that he is also walking out on himself.

A few years ago a gentleman whom I knew quite well was taken ill. Goaded by his pain, he went to see his physician. But it so happened that the physician's waiting room was crowded. My friend settled down to wait, but he was short on patience. The longer he waited, the more angry he became. He stood it for a few hours because he felt he might be looking the undertaker eye to eye. At last he stalked out in rage. By his foolish conduct he convinced all his friends that he reached the cemetery ahead of time.

In everyday English we call this giving way to rage "getting mad." It is a fitting word. As a rule, when we lose our tempers, we also lose our sanity as well. We cease to act rationally. For the moment we park our intelligence and act as if we were insane. I have known a man in a fit of temper to lash out at a fine piece of machinery and wreck it. I have known another with the same lack of sanity to wreck a friendship and yet another to spoil his marriage. Even so, this fine gentleman with superb insanity turned and went away.

I

This man who lost his temper was named Naaman. The author of II Kings has some very complimentary things to say about him.

1. He was a great man with his master, and his master was a king. Naaman, therefore, moved in the atmosphere of royalty. Being thus intimate with his king, he was a man of high social position. To be invited into his home was to become a part of the elect four hundred of that day. He was also a man of political influence. For one seeking a position, to have his backing was the best possible guarantee of success in getting it.

2. Not only was Naaman a man of high social and political position, but he was a man of substance. Of course there are many things that money cannot buy. But there are so many things that it can buy that the Bible never speaks of money with contempt. When Naaman set out to see the prophet, he took with him ten talents of silver and six thousand shekels of gold. That was a fortune. Had

he turned all that over to Elisha, it would have made him independently rich. Naaman was a man of substance.

3. Naaman was a military hero. He was in a sense the "father of his country." He was held in high honor by his people. We have always honored those who wear the uniform. Sometimes for obvious reasons and sometimes for reasons not so obvious. At the close of the Spanish-American War we were a little short on heroes. But there was one who was outstanding. That was Lieutenant Richmond P. Hobson. So highly honored was he that, when he returned home, at every station he was greeted by crowds of ladies who insisted upon giving him a kiss. I have never known whether to envy or pity him. I have an idea that some of those who thus favored him had not been kissed for a long time. Now I do not know whether Naaman got any extra kisses or not, but I do know that he deserved them. He was a great military hero.

4. Finally, he was a mighty man of valor. That is, I take it, he was courageous. Courage is one virtue that is universally admired. Some may have no patience with patience. But everybody admires courage. It is admired by the old and the young, by the cultured and the uncultured. It is admired in the Occident and in the Orient, by those of yesterday and by those of today. So important is courage that if I were to write a book about a friend and fill every page with compliments, then add at the last part of the last page these words "but he is a coward," it would spoil my hero. Naaman was a man of courage.

But having enumerated all these fine assets, the author is unable to give Naaman a clean bill of health. He says that he was all these things—but. As a student in Latin at Webb School, I learned to parse that word. It is an adversative conjunction. What a fitting name! That is, it goes against all that has been said before. Even if we do not know how to parse it, we usually know how to use it in a telling fashion.

For instance, if we desire to say something passingly ugly about our friend, we simply say it. But if we desire to give him an especially heavy jolt, we preface that with a compliment. "That certainly is a beautiful car George is driving," I say to a friend. "But if he were to pay his debts, he would be on foot or, at best, driving a jalopy." Even so, Naaman had wealth, position—almost everything "but." But what? But he was a leper.

Now at the risk of seeming trite I am going to dare to be tragic. I could say much about every one of us that would not only be gracious and complimentary but also true. But having said all that is lovely, in order to be loyal to the facts I would have to add, "We have all these treasures, but." But what? But many of us are still strangers to the life abundant. We have failed to receive that spirit of power and love and of healthy-mindedness that can only come from God through Christ. Therefore, though we may not be tortured by any deep sense of guilt, we still are tortured by an inward lack that has left us little better than spiritual invalids.

How this ghastly disease stole upon Naaman we are not told. But probably one day when he went to consult the royal physician, that gentleman ducked behind some scientific term that might mean anything or nothing.

Short-tempered Naaman saw that he was dodging. "Tell me the truth," he urged. "I'm no baby."

"Well," answered the physician, "if you must know, you have leprosy."

"Leprosy! that ghastly disease of which beggars rot in the mouths of caves?"

"Yes," said the physician, "also the ghastly disease that drags kings from their thrones. You have leprosy. Furthermore, I regret to have to tell you that there is little or nothing I can do. I have no cure for leprosy."

Therefore, in spite of all his fine assets, there was a shadow over the life of Naaman. There was also a shadow over his home. Even the little slave girl who had been taken in a raid upon Israel knew that there was something wrong. Therefore, in spite of the fact that she had suffered at the hands of Naaman and his people, she could not help sharing their suffering. So she said to her mistress, "I wish that my master would visit the prophet who is in Samaria. He would cure him of his leprosy."

Naturally Naaman's wife was all interest. "You say your prophet can cure my husband?" she questioned.

"I am perfectly sure of it," she answered.

"Did he ever cure anyone?" the wife continued.

"Not so far as I know," she had to answer.

"Then perhaps there are no lepers in Israel," the wife continued.

"There are many," replied the girl, "but so far they have not had the faith to be cured."

That was not too encouraging; yet when the general came home, his wife told him what the little girl had said. But he showed no enthusiasm. "If this prophet has never cured anyone, why should I go to him?"

"Well," she replied, "if you stay here, the doctor promises you nothing. If you go to see the prophet, there might be a chance. Failure is at least not a certainty. Why not give yourself a chance even if it seems small?" Whatever indecision might still have tormented Naaman was ended by no less a personage than the king himself. Feeling that the general was too good a man to lose, he urged him to visit the prophet.

II

Then came the setting out. Naaman went with the pomp and pageantry that became one of his rank. He did not set out like a leper seeking a cure but rather like a prince going to receive his crown. He went not only armed with abundant cash but with a letter to the king of Israel. Of course it would have been beneath his dignity to approach one of lesser rank.

This letter read a bit after this fashion: This will introduce to you my servant Naaman, who comes to be cured of his leprosy. When the king read that, it frightened him half out of his wits. "Am I God," he said, "to kill and to make alive?" In sheer desperation he tore his royal robes.

Meantime the news of Naaman's arrival reached Elisha. "Send him to me," he urged. At that Naaman set out on the second lap of his journey. All his military pride and snobbery were alert and alive. I can imagine that he smiled inwardly as he thought how excited this prophet was going to be when he saw his important visitor. Not only so, but as he went to the parsonage, he made out a kind of blueprint of the way he was going to be cured. For being as important as he was, he felt he must be cured on his own terms. Here is how it was going to work. "As soon as I am announced, the prophet will come out. He will stand, of course, with due humility. He will next call upon his God. Then he will wave his hand over me, go through a kind of hocus-pocus, and I shall be cured."

But it did not work out that way. When he reached the parsonage, he perhaps sent a servant in to tell of his arrival. "General Naaman is without," announced the servant, "waiting to be cured of his leprosy." "Yes," replied the prophet, "I was expecting him. Tell him to go dip in Jordan seven times and he will be cured."

Armed with that good news, the servant hurried out to tell his master. He was thrilled that the way to recovery was so simple, so down to earth. But before he could speak, the general broke in. "Where is that prophet?"

"He is sitting in there," came the answer.

"Isn't he coming out?"

"He didn't look as if he were."

"Well, what did he say?"

"He said all you had to do to be cured was to go dip in Jordan seven times."

"Ridiculous," thundered Naaman. "Drive on," he ordered. "I am going home. I am not going to be insulted in any such fashion." But before he had gone far, I can imagine that I, an old friend and fellow graduate of West Point, run into him.

"Hello, General," I greet him. "What in the world are you doing in Samaria?"

"I came to be cured of my affliction," he answers. "I was told that there was a prophet down here who could heal me. But I have had all my pains for nothing, so I am going back home."

"Too bad that the prophet is a fake," I answer, "or maybe he is unwilling to help because you are an outsider."

"No," replies the general, "it was not like that. You see, I had made up my mind as to how I was going to be cured, but he did not cure me that way. Furthermore, he told me to go dip in this muddy Jordan when anybody knows the rivers of Damascus are far better. He so outraged my pride that I decided to go home."

"But," I persist, "have you given his remedy a trial? Even if it fails, you will be none the worse; but if you refuse, there is no hope of a cure."

"Well, I do refuse," he replies. "You see, he punctured my pride by not curing me in my way. Then he insulted me by putting Jordan above the rivers of Damascus. In short, he made me mad. Therefore I am going back home. This I am doing in spite of that fact that I know that getting mad at the prophet is a poor cure for leprosy."

That was silly enough, but Naaman is not the only man who ever sought physical or spiritual healing on his own terms.

III

Then comes the turning point in the story. A wise and devoted servant dared to make a suggestion. This servant had doubtless been in the household of Naaman for a long time. I have an idea that he was quite well acquainted with the little Jewish maiden who had started Naaman on his quest. I should not wonder if he had not come to share her finer faith. Be that as it may, in tender earnestness he dared to ask the angry general this very sane question.

"My father, if the prophet had commanded you to do some great thing, would you not have done it?"

"How is that?" answered the general.

"Suppose the prophet had demanded of you every penny that you have in the world, wouldn't you have given it?"

"Certainly. All that a man has he will give for his life."

"If he had called on you to do something conspicuous, even impossible, such as crawling all the way back to Damascus on your hands and knees, wouldn't you have tried that? How much rather then when he tells you to do something so simple that it is as truly within the reach of a little child as it is of a king on his throne!"

At that the good sense of Naaman asserted itself. He decided to take the prescription. I can see him as he walks into the waters of the Jordan while his faithful servant watches on the bank. He then humbly dips himself once, then a second time, and then a third. But nothing happens. "I am just as leprous as I was at the beginning," he tells his servant.

"But you have not yet gone the whole way," comes the sane reply. "Seven times. Remember?"

So he counts them off. He has now dipped six times with no difference. Then he takes the final plunge. At that the servant rubs his eyes in amazement and gladness. The impossible has taken place. For "his flesh was restored like the flesh of a little child." A picture of the ever-old and ever-new story of life made over.

Now what was it that brought Naaman's healing? It was not the waters of the Jordan. What was it that made Paul a new creation in Christ Jesus, that enabled him to sing, "The old has passed away, behold, the new has come"? It was not, as we generally suppose, that vision that blinded him on the way from Jerusalem to Damascus. Paul might have gone from the shining of that light into a deeper darkness than he had ever known before. What was it that saved him? Here is the answer in his own words: "I was not disobedient to the heavenly vision." Even so, Naaman was healed because he dared to obey.

That is the way of healing for all of us, and there is none other. One day Jesus stopped beside the worn pallet of a man who had lain flat on his back for half a lifetime. He asked this man what at first seems a rather amazing question. This is the question, "Do you want to get well?" That question implied at least three facts that intimately concerned this sick man. In fact, they concern every man.

First, Jesus was saying to this invalid what the sick man certainly would have said to himself. "You are sick; there is something wrong with you." A second fact that Jesus affirmed is: "Though you are sick, though you have been out of the game for thirty-eight years, you do not have to remain out. You can still be well and take your place in the world of men." Third: "If you are to get well, you must put yourself absolutely in my hands. If you give yourself to me in complete obedience, I will make you whole."

It so happens that I belong to the "aristocracy of the operated." I wish I could tell you about my operation. It is an exciting story. I think some of the most impatient moments of my life have been spent listening to some friend tell how he felt just as he was coming out of the anesthetic. Of course the story was interesting, but my impatience grew out of the fact that I was eager for him to get through so I could tell how I felt when I was coming out from the anesthetic.

But in all seriousness, it takes an amazing faith to go through a difficult surgical operation. How much confidence I had to have in my physician to lie down and sleep a sleep that was for the moment as deep as death, when I knew that one false move on his part might send me into eternity! But I so trusted. Not only so, but I rejoice to say that my faith was not disappointed.

No human physician can cure all the patients who come to him. The best of them fail many times. But there is a Physician who never fails. All he needs to work his cure is just an opportunity. If you are not enjoying vigorous spiritual health, there is a way out. There is an open road to the life abundant for every man. That is the road of dedication, of obedience. For "if any man's will is to do his will, he shall know."

12

The Man Who Majored in Gratitude

Give thanks in all circumstances.
I Thess. 5:18

Paul was a master of the fine art of appreciation. He is conspicuous in this respect even among the writers of the Bible. That is indeed a high claim. This is the case because to open this Book is to come upon a company of radiant souls whose faces fairly shine with the joy of gratitude. It is to hear a great chorus choir engaged in singing songs of thanksgiving. But among all these voices the most conspicuous, I think, is that of this apostle. Both by his life and by his lips he was constantly saying, "Give thanks in all circumstances."

I

Why is Paul so eager that we learn the fine art of appreciation?

1. He is eager because he knows that gratitude is a mark of mental and moral growth. We do not expect appreciation from little babies, but we do expect it from adults. A brilliant woman of more than a generation ago tells of a young and wealthy friend of hers who became the wife of an equally wealthy man. For eight or ten

years she lost sight of this beautiful and dear friend. Then one day as she was walking down Fifth Avenue in New York, she saw her disappear through the door of a brownstone mansion. She hurried on eager feet to ring that doorbell. At first there was no response. Then her friend opened.

"Hello, Anne," said the visitor. "I have not seen you for years. Where have you been?"

"Come in and I'll tell you," came the answer.

When the visitor had entered, her friend led her up a carved stairway and into a nursery that was fitted with oriental luxury. There in a baby pen was a boy some eight years of age. He was a ghastly, drooling idiot.

"That is what I have been doing," said her friend. "He is my baby. I have given my life to him, and I am glad to give it." Then in spite of herself the look of defiant pride melted into one of unspeakable sorrow and wistfulness as she said, "Yes, I'm glad to give my life to him. But, oh, Jane, it would be so much easier if he could tell me from you. After all these years he doesn't even know that I am his mother."

Well, God has children like that. Gratitude is a mark of mental and moral growth.

2. Gratitude is a source of joy. It is a source of joy to its possessor. It does not matter how full life may have filled your fortunate hands; if with your wealth you have no gratitude, no appreciation, you are still a pauper. But it is equally true that, however empty your hands may be, however many treasures sorrow and misfortune may have wrenched from them, if you have a firm hold upon grati-

tude, you are still unspeakably rich. Gratitude is a source of joy to its possessor.

Not only so, but it is a source at once of joy and help to those to whom we express it. In fact, I do not know of any way that we can do so much good with such a small output as we can by being grateful. A friend said to Job, "Your words have upheld him who was stumbling." I have an idea they were words of appreciation. You have been kept from stumbling by such words, as I have. Not only so, but under the inspiration of such words we have moved toward richer and fuller lives. This is the case because we bloom into our best in an atmosphere of appreciation as naturally as flowers bloom at the kiss of springtime.

Gratitude is a gift that everybody needs and that everybody can give. In *The House Beautiful,* Channing Pollock tells the story of a wife who was married to quite a commonplace husband. To others he seemed little more than a creature of clay. But she saw him through eyes made clear by appreciation. Therefore, when day by day he came home from his ordinary task, her face would take on a new radiance. "Don't you hear the bugles blowing?" she would ask. "That is for my knight. He is coming home from the battle." Naturally that husband moved toward greatness. It is next to impossible to remain little under the power of an appreciation like that.

There are thousands today who are walking with lagging steps, who are looking out on life with lackluster eyes, who would have a new spring in their step and a new sparkle in their glance if those who live with them and who actually appreciate them would give expression to that appreciation.

Across the years it has been my lot to hold many a funeral. Not once have I had a desperate soul to grasp my hands and look at me with dry eyes that could not weep and say, "I was too thoughtful and too appreciative of this dear one who has passed." But how many funerals I have held when I knew that the greatest sorrow was the fact that the one who mourned was trying to say to the dead what he knew he ought to have said to the living! Therefore, when I realize how much more smoothly the friction-fretted machinery of everyday life would run if it were oiled a little more liberally and a little more frequently by this fine lubricant of appreciation, and when I realize further that it does not cost a penny a carload, I wonder that I do not make a larger use of it.

II

Now, since gratitude is a treasure and since it is a means of giving needed help, to refuse to give such help is a sin against God and man. "Whoever knows what is right to do and fails to do it, for him it is sin." Therefore when Paul said, "Give thanks in all circumstances," he was giving most excellent advice. But it is far more than good advice; it is a command. It is a command that is enjoined over and over again throughout both the Old and the New Testaments.

The fact that it is a command means this, at least: that we can be grateful; that if we are not grateful, it is not so much our misfortune as it is our sin. I know that we find it hard to believe this. So many of us are convinced that gratitude is purely a matter of circumstances. If everything comes right side up, naturally we are grateful. But if suffering and loss and disappointment come, then we are quite as naturally ungrateful. Not only so, but our ingratitude is entirely justified.

But this is not the case at all. Gratitude is not born of our circumstances; it is a child of the heart. Therefore when Paul said, "Give thanks in all circumstances," he was laying upon us a command that by the grace of God we can obey. He himself had obeyed it across the years. He was speaking out of his own experience. He had been grateful in every sort of situation, the blackest as well as the brightest. For instance, in his second letter to the Corinthians he cannot find much in those disappointing saints for which to be grateful. They had all but broken his heart. But though he could not commend them, he still thanks God for them. This is the case because he has learned through the heartache that they have caused him something of the power of God to comfort.

Here he is on a mission to Philippi. But what a dismal failure that mission turned out to be! He was not followed by eager throngs. Instead, he and his companion were seized in the street; their clothes were torn from their bodies; and they were shamefully whipped. Then, with their bleeding backs, they were thrust into the inner part of a stenchful prison and their feet were made fast in the stocks. But instead of wailing they sang so joyfully that their fellow prisoners found their songs irresistible. They were abounding in gratitude. But their thankfulness was no more born of circumstances than was that of their Lord, of whom we read: "He took a cup, and when he had given thanks"—our Christ was thankful even for the privilege of being hung on a cross for our redemption.

Now since we can be grateful in all circumstances, to refuse to be, I repeat, is a sin. It is one of the most cruel of sins. If I refuse to give you bread when I myself am starving, there would be some excuse. But if I refuse you the bread of appreciation when by giving it I could enrich both myself and you, that would be sheer devilishness. The high-water mark of English tragedy is *King Lear*. In this story a cruel daughter is teaching a doting father "how sharper than a serpent's tooth it is to have a thankless child." Ingratitude is one of the most cruel and common of sins.

III

"Give thanks in all circumstances." How are we to obey this command?

1. Let us cultivate the habit of looking at what we have instead of at what we have missed. Some people get their gaze so fixed on what they have missed that they fail to see what they have. One of my tasks as a boy was to feed the hogs. I have carried a basketful of shucked corn, perhaps a hundred ears, and poured it all out together. Every hog could have had at least three or four ears for his very own. But instead of acting as if that were the case, one silly pig would grab a single ear and dart off up the hill as if death were at his heels. What was more amazing still, often three or four other pigs, weeping and wailing,

would run after him, as if he had the one ear that was worth eating. How like folks!

It was my joyful privilege to know that rare preacher and spiritual genius Bud Robinson. Once a friend spent a whole day showing Bud over the great and gripping city of New York. When they had returned late at night to their hotel, this friend overheard Bud saying his prayers. "Lord," he prayed, "I just want to thank you that I ain't seen a single thing that I want." How rich he was! Some folks can't even go window-shopping without coming home miserable. If we are going to be grateful, we must look at what we have instead of at what we have missed. That was Paul's way. He commended it to us. "If there is anything worthy of praise, think about these things."

2. If we are going to be grateful, we must look at what we have in the light of the facts. We must look with eyes that see. Thus we shall realize with Paul that everything we have came to us primarily as a gift. "What have you that you did not receive?" I know that we have worked. We have bent our shoulders under heavy tasks. But who gave us the capacity to work? Who gave us a task at which to work? Who gave us a world with great and thrilling opportunities? All that came as a gift. If God were to take out of our hands at this moment everythng except that for which we are solely responsible, nothing would be left, not even our hands.

What was the matter with the rich farmer? Why did Jesus call him a fool? It was not because he made money. It was not because he made money dishonestly. He had made it in the cleanest and most honorable fashion. It was not because he had sought to conserve what he made. That was sensible. To waste is wicked. He showed his foolishness in what he forgot. He forgot God. Therefore he thought that to possess a farm is to own one. Thus owning a farm, he was at once without obligation and without gratitude. Naturally our Lord called him a fool. There was no other name that would adequately describe a man who had no one to thank but himself.

Yet how often it is true that the less responsible we are for our blessings, the more we tend to swagger over them. I do not think that I have known many men who were conceited because they could make money, but I am sure that I have known quite a few who were conceited because they could inherit it. Yet that does not require any great genius. Or take physical beauty. That is no mean gift, but gift it is. Yet the most beautiful girl I ever knew impressed me as being about the most ungrateful and selfish. As a result she could not endure hearing any other girl complimented. No friend of hers could even be an also-ran. Therefore not many wept when a few years later she took on weight. If we are to be grateful, we are to face the fact that all we have came as a gift.

3. If we are to be grateful, we must see something special in the gifts that have been put into our hands and into our hearts. There are few swear words more ugly than the words "of course," when wrongly used. For instance, when one told the poet Heine that God would forgive him, he gave this devilish answer, "Of course, that is his business."

"God's house is open to you this holy Sabbath," I remind you.

"Of course," you reply, "it is open every Sabbath."

"Behold, I stand at the door and knock," I continue.

"Of course," you often reply. "He knocked yesterday. He will doubtless knock again tomorrow." Thus those horrid words have struck the death blow to gratitude countless thousands of times.

It lays its destroying hands on our relationships with each other. I know a man who has been taken captive by drink. His wife has borne with him, followed him with her patience and her prayers through the years. When seeking to win him, I remind him of this. If he says, "Of course," I rate my chances of helping him very low indeed. There is something special in the devotion of your wife, the devotion of your husband, the devotion of your parents. There is even something special about that teen-age boy who knows everything, it seems, except how to be grateful. Yet even he might cease one day to say "Of course" and return with understanding to say "Thank you."

Often we even take the rich gift of life for granted. Years ago my young nephew was sharing his wisdom with me concerning the uncertainty of life. He informed me that he did not know whether he would live another year or not. Then he shortened the time and said, "I do not know whether I will live another month or not," and I had to agree. Then he said with great emphasis, "When I go to bed at night, I do not know whether I will be alive in the morning or not." To this I also agreed. Then he added these significant words, "I'm so used to getting up without being dead that I don't intend to die." In other words, when he woke in the morning, his first words were, "Of course." He saw nothing special in the gift of a new day.

4. Finally, if we are going to be grateful, we must give expression to our gratitude. I know how hard it is for some of us to do that. We are a bit timid and diffident. We tell ourselves, "She knows how much I appreciate her." "He knows how much I appreciate him." But how? Besides, even those who do know like to hear it. Even God himself is no exception. Therefore he urges, "Let the redeemed of the Lord say so."

If we give expression to our gratitude, it will grow from more to more. If we shut it up in our hearts, it will die. Paul refused to run this risk. He constantly cultivated the fine art of appreciation by giving it expression. So persistent was he in saying "Thank you" both to God and to man that it became a habit. His gratitude became increasingly natural and spontaneous. It was as spontaneous as the gushing of a spring, as the song of a bird, as the laughter of a happy child. For this reason I feel that none save Paul's Master is better fitted to call us to this high duty and privilege, "Give thanks in all circumstances."

13

The Man Who Amazed Jesus

When Jesus heard this he marveled at him, and turned and said . . . , "I tell you, not even in Israel have I found such faith."
Luke 7:9

Only twice in the Gospels are we told that Jesus was made to marvel. Once when he was visiting his home town, eager to do great things, he was able to accomplish but little. This was due, not to any lack on his part, but to a lack of faith on the part of his fellow villagers. So we read that he marveled at their unbelief. He was amazed that having so much in the way of opportunity they made so little of it. But here he is amazed that this Roman officer with so little in the way of opportunity made so much of it. He marveled at the richness and fullness of his faith.

I

Look at the distant background. Here I confess that I am depending largely on my imagination. As a senior officer in the army, I imagine that I meet this young centurion on the streets of Rome. "Have you heard the news?" he questions with eager enthusiasm. "I have just received an appointment to foreign service. All my service so far has been here at home. I am now going to be stationed at Capernaum, in the land of the Jews. It is my first chance of this kind, and I can hardly wait to be at my task."

Being older and more cynical, I look at this young chap with a mingling of envy and pity. "Well," I reply, "I congratulate you. But in all honesty I cannot make my congratulations as hearty as I should like. You see, I spent some time with the army of occupation in Capernaum. I found that in spite of the fact that those Jews have been conquered they are still vastly proud. Indeed, they look upon us Romans as Gentile dogs. They heartily hate us! Therefore they spare themselves no effort to make our task as unpleasant as possible. My one bit of advice to you is, show them from the beginning who is master. If you give them an inch, they will take a whole mile."

As the young captain continued his way down the street, there was perhaps not quite so much spring in his step or light in his eye as before this meeting. But being young and hopeful, he did not stay depressed long. Therefore, when a few months later he found himelf at his post in Capernaum, he must have forgotten the importance of being a bully. I can imagine that, thus forgetting, he was surprised that these proud people whom he had come to rule with no right except that of might showed so little hostility.

In fact, before he had been there many months, I can picture some hardened Simon coming from transacting certain business with the young captain and saying to himself and to no one else, "I believe he likes me." By and by he had the courage to confess as much to one of his fellows who had also had dealings with this captain. "Yes," answered his friend, "I also believe that he likes me." Then they almost inevitably took the next step. Though they may not have confessed it openly, each said, "I like him, too."

We may be sure of this because there is an echo between human hearts as there is an echo in nature. As a plowboy I used to shout to a rugged cliff that stood just across the river from where I worked. I found that I could get any response from that cliff that I desired. If I happened to be in an evil mood and wanted to have my ears knocked down, all I had to do was to tell this cliff. On the other hand, if I desired a bit of boosting, all that was necessary was for me to boost the cliff. Jesus put it in these words: "The measure you give will be the measure you get."

There is abiding truth in the story of those two pioneer families that years ago were moving west to a new settlement. When the first of these neared their destination, they met a man on horseback. The father asked him the name of the next settlement. When he was informed that it was the goal of their journey, he asked another question. "What kind of people live there?"

"What kind did you leave?" the stranger replied.

"What kind did I leave?" came the bitter answer. "They were such a disagreeable lot that we could not live with them. That is the reason for our moving out here."

"Well," came the reply, "I am sorry to tell you, but

you will find the same kind of people where you are going."

A little later, when the second pioneer met the same gentleman, he asked the same questions—the name of the settlement and then the kind of people who lived there. The stranger also gave the same response: "What kind of people did you leave?"

"They were just the dearest people in the world," came the reply. "It fairly broke our hearts to leave them."

"Well," answered the stranger, "you can go on your way with confidence. You will find the same kind of people where you are going."

There was every reason that these Jews should have hated this Roman official. They were divided from him by about the widest possible chasms. They were divided by the wide chasm of race. They were divided by the wide chasm of religion. They were divided by the wide chasm of conquered and conqueror. But so did this young captain conduct himself toward them that at last he compelled them to say, "He loves us." What an unbelievable triumph!

Did he become a convert to their faith? We are not told. I am inclined to believe that he did. As so many intelligent Romans of that day, he had doubtless broken with the religion of his fathers. He had become disgusted with gods that were so lustful and vengeful that they were far beneath the standards of human decency. The conception of one God held by these Jews appealed to him. There was an even stronger appeal in the fact that this God, at once holy and fatherly, required nothing of his people except that they do justly, love kindness, and walk in humble fellowship with himself.

Even if he did not come out openly as a convert, he so believed in their faith that he desired to promote it. When, therefore, they needed a new church, he insisted that he be allowed to build it out of his own pocket. That was of course a bit dangerous. Generally speaking, the members of a church love it in proportion to the way they sacrifice for it. But we may be sure that this Roman was seeking in the best way that he knew to be helpful. Thus he won a place in the hearts of people that had every reason to hate him. So much for the distant background.

II

Now for the near background.

One day tragedy struck. It came through the desperate illness of a dearly loved slave. Here again we get a glimpse of the brotherliness of this official. He had not only bridged the chasm between race and race, between one religion and another, between conqueror and conquered, but between master and slave. This sick man was dear to him, not as chattel, but as a friend. Naturally, therefore, when sickness came, he went into action on his friend's behalf. We may be sure that he secured for him the best physicians of Capernaum. But in spite of all their ministrations the patient grew steadily worse. Then it was that this official heard of Jesus.

I think we may be sure that this was not the first time he had heard of this amazing Prophet. I love to imagine that this official knew that nobleman who lived in Capernaum. This man had gone to Jesus on behalf of his sick son and had not gone in vain. This, together with all else that he had heard of Jesus, convinced him of two facts: first, that this prophet was willing to help; second, that he was not only willing but able. What he had heard at the present moment, I think, was that Jesus was now near enough to be accessible. He perhaps learned that he was in or near Capernaum.

Convinced, then, of the willingness, the ability, and nearness of Jesus, he betook himself to prayer for the healing of his slave. But in presenting his petition, he did not go to the Master in person. He sent to him elders of the Jews. This he did, but not because he was too busy to go himself. No more did he send them because he, as a Roman conqueror, was too proud to ask a favor of a Jewish peasant. He did not go in person because of his deep humility. This officer was not poor-spirited. We may count on that. But he was "poor in spirit." Therefore he sent to Jesus men whom he considered more worthy than himself.

If it amazes us that out of humility he sent these elders, it is equally amazing that they on their part were willing to go. Were they themselves disciples? We are not told. I hardly think so. However, they did believe that Jesus could do works of healing. I think they went out of sheer friendship. Having come into the presence of Jesus, they did not present their petition in a lukewarm fashion. Their attitude was not one of merely saying, "We have done our part; take it or leave it." Instead, they were in dead earnest. They put their best into their prayer. "He is worthy to have you do this for him," they pleaded. "He loves our nation, and he built us our synagogue."

Here are two estimates of the same man: "I am not worthy to have you come under my roof; therefore I did not presume to come to you." So this humble-hearted man spoke of himself. But his friends, those friends whom he had won by sheer good will, had a finer estimate: "He is worthy," they affirmed with conviction. It is true, even among men, that "everyone who exalts himself will be humbled, and he who humbles himself will be exalted." The man who is deeply in love with his own bigness will usually have no rival. Now when these came thus pleading the cause of their friend, they did not come in vain. Jesus responded to their earnest prayer and at once set out on this mission of healing.

III

In the final scene this captain again did the utterly unexpected. I can see him sitting by the bedside of his slave, perhaps holding his thin hand that is now growing cold. He looks out the window and sees Jesus approaching. In his place I should certainly have sprung to my feet and hurried out to urge, "Be quick, he is almost gone." But this officer did the very opposite. He called some friends and sent them in hot haste with this message, "Lord, do not trouble yourself." How contradictory! "Come," he once urged. Now it is, "Do not come."

Why is he acting in this strange fashion? It is certainly not because he has lost hope. Instead, he is very sure. He takes this course, first, out of humility. Then, he takes it because he is convinced that the coming of Jesus is not necessary. This man did not require any sort of visible prop to hold up his faith. He did not ask for the physical presence of Jesus. He did not ask even for a promise. He staked his all on the personality of the Master himself. He was sure that Jesus, being the kind of man he was, could and would heal his slave.

What a thrilling faith! But we are not to think of it as mere credulity. He did not believe because he had made his judgment blind. Instead, he had thought things through —hours, maybe days and weeks before. He had thus reached a faith that to me seems altogether rational. Though conscious of the infinite distance that separated him from the Master, he saw that in some respects they were alike.

Therefore, in giving a reason for his faith he said, "I am a man set under authority, with soldiers under me: and I say to one, 'Go,' and he goes; and to another, 'Come,' and he comes." That is, being under authority, he can speak with authority. The source of his authority was first his superior officer. But the final source was none other than the emperor himself. Being thus under the authority of the emperor, he could speak with the authority of the emperor, indeed of the whole Roman Empire.

"Now just as I am under the authority of the emperor," this man reasoned, "even so Jesus is under the authority of Almighty God. He acts under infinite authority; therefore, he can speak with infinite authority." What a fine insight! No wonder Jesus was thrilled. It penetrated to a truth that Jesus himself proclaimed: "I can do nothing on my own authority." The secret of the power of our Lord is his perfect dedication to the will of God. It is true that we ourselves can speak with authority in proportion to the fullness with which we submit to the authority of Almighty God.

What came of his so sane, so rational, so firm faith? There could be only one answer. When these friends returned from their mission, they found the slave well. Such a faith never is and never can be disappointing.

IV

Was this centurion a Christian?

Whether he ever made such claim by his lips, we are not told. But by his life he put himself among the choicest of the saints. He possessed those characteristics that belong to the Christian at his best everywhere and in every age.

First, he was a man of beautiful humility. He was one of the "poor in spirit" to whom the doors of the kingdom opened of their own accord. Had he gone into the temple to pray, he would not have stood up with the Pharisee to congratulate God on having so splendid a servant as himself. Instead, he would have taken his stand beside the publican who felt himself so unfit that God was able to send him down to his house transformed.

Second, he was a helpful man. He was a man whose prayers could release the power of God upon a given situation or a given individual. Under God this slave owed his life to him. He was that type of believer of whom Jesus was speaking when he said, "Out of his heart shall flow rivers of living water." This man was of that elect group who break up the drought of the soul and set the fields of the heart to flowering.

Finally, he was a man of an invincible good will. Jesus gave only one acid test of discipleship. Strange as it may seem to some, that test has nothing to do with our particular denomination or the mode of our baptism. Here is his test: "By this all men will know that you are my disciples, if you have love for one another." If this is the hallmark of a real Christian, then this centurion certainly found his way into the feast of the fullness of life.

This good will is not only essential to vital Christianity but to the salvation of the world. The man who exercised it in his fullest died on a cross. But he died believing that love is stronger than hate, that lifted up from the earth he would draw all men unto himself. Such good will has never really been tried among the nations. But when tried between man and man, it has worked when all else has failed.

A friend told me of this event that took place in his own city. A gentleman who was a practicing Christian and a man of considerable substance bought a lovely old estate in the suburbs of that city and proceeded to have repairs made. Being a very busy man, he did not appear on the scene until late one afternoon. He was standing on his wide lawn when his next-door neighbor saw him. At once this man hurried out through his own front gate and through that of the newcomer. Without any introduction he proceeded to speak to him in this ugly fashion: "Did you buy this? If you did, I want to tell you that you have bought a hunk of trouble. You have bought a lawsuit. That fence is five feet over on my land. I am going to have all of what is mine if it costs me every penny I have. So you might as well get ready for trouble."

The newcomer looked at his angry neighbor with quiet eyes, then answered, "My friend, I see no necessity for trouble, nor is there any need for a lawsuit. Though I bought this land in good faith, I can see that you are perfectly sincere in claiming that my fence is over on your land. That being the case, I promise to have it moved the first thing in the morning. I would have it moved now, but my workmen are gone."

"What did you say?" the angry neighbor asked in bewilderment. "You mean to tell me that you are going to have that fence moved the first thing in the morning?"

"That is exactly what I mean," came the quite serious answer.

"Blankety, blank, blank! No you won't," was the reply. "That fence stays right where it is; that is, unless you wish to put it five feet farther over on my land. Anybody who will answer me as you did after I made the approach that I made to you can have the whole estate if he wants it." So these two who might have become bitter enemies became warm friends.

But the supreme fact about this centurion was his amazing faith. That was what made all else possible. He has a place among the great believers. Thus believing in God, he was a man of rare humility. The man with a real sense of God in his life is always humble. His faith gave him power. His faith increased and enriched his good will. I do not wonder that Jesus marveled at him as he rejoiced over him. Countless thousands of others, as the centuries have come and gone, have felt their hearts strangely warmed in his presence. We look at him at this hour and thank God for the privilege of sharing his rich and enriching faith.

14

The Man Who Gave Way to Hate

He immediately went out; and it was night.
John 13:30

"It was night." That is a haunting sentence. We cannot read it intelligently without a shudder. As we listen, we hear more than words; we hear the steps of Judas as he descends the stairs through the night to betray his Lord. We also hear him as he descends an invisible stairway to an immortality of shame. This deed, I daresay, has made his name the best known among the twelve. I think there are those who are familiar with the name of Judas and that for which it stands who would not know either Peter or James or John. But in spite of the fact that we know the name of Judas so well, I feel we know Judas the man far too little.

I

Why is this the case?

I think it is due to the fact that we have judged him by only one single deed of his life, and that the worst he ever committed. We have fixed our gaze on only one single picture of his face. That is one portraying the leer of a traitor. Now it is a fact that Judas betrayed his Lord, but that is not all that he did. He went on missions with his fellow disciples. So far as the record goes, he acquitted himself as well as they. Then, too, he was the treasurer of the little group. He dispensed their charities. I have an idea that he dispensed them wisely and well. There were, therefore, doubtless scores and even hundreds who had been helped by Judas and who called his name in their prayers of thanksgiving.

In saying this, I am not agreeing with those who affirm that Judas was not at heart a traitor. There are those who argue that he really believed in Jesus more profoundly than his fellows. He was such a firm believer that he dared to put his Master on the spot with the assurance that he would then assert his divine power. Naturally every right-thinking person would be glad to believe this, but there is no evidence of its truth. The friends of Judas, including his Master, never spoke of him as a mistaken man who did a foolish thing. Always he is pictured as a treacherous man who did a devilish thing. Thus he discovered long before Bunyan that hard by the gate of heaven there is a by-way to hell.

Still, in judging Judas by one single deed, we have done him great injustice. Sometime ago two lovely girls from my state disputed a railroad crossing with an oncoming train. The result was that their youthful bodies were so mangled they had to be picked up in baskets. Suppose, after the undertaker had done his best, I should have looked into their caskets and said, "What horrible creatures!" "Oh, no," everyone would answer, "that is not fair. You only saw them after the wreck." Even so, the vast majority only see Judas after the wreck.

II

What then can we say of Judas the man? There are three assertions we can make about him on which I believe we can agree.

1. Judas was not born a traitor. When his mother looked into his baby eyes, she saw nothing of treachery. This was the case because babies are not so much born as made. Nobody is ever born a traitor, just as nobody is ever born a saint. I know there are those who misquote the Scriptures and thus affirm that Judas was a devil from the beginning. But the Scriptures say no such thing. Nobody was ever a devil from the beginning, not even the Devil himself.

It is true that some ten or twelve months before Calvary, Jesus said, "Did I not choose you, the twelve, and one of you is a devil?" What did he mean by this harsh word? Did he mean that Judas had become an incarnate fiend? What did he mean when, after his great confession, he said a similar word to Simon? "Get behind me, Satan." Had Simon become altogether bad? Not a bit of it. No more had Judas. This man began as an innocent baby. He became a traitor. But, to the very end, there was so much of good in him that he found it impossible to live with himself.

2. A second fact upon which we can all agree is that Judas, of his own choice, became a disciple. He is accused of being a lover of money. I have an idea that the

accusation is true. Assuming that it is, one day this young man, a lover of things, encountered Jesus. How they met we are not told. But one eventful hour they came face to face, and Judas could never forget that meeting. The presence and personality of this amazing young prophet haunted him.

No doubt there was much about Jesus that repelled Judas. He perhaps impressed this very practical man as being too flighty. He did not quite have his feet on the ground. Judas was offended by the fact that Jesus was a confessed son of poverty. He was further offended by the exacting demands Jesus made upon his followers, calling upon them to forsake their all to become his disciples. But in spite of all this, so tremendous was the spell that Jesus cast over Judas that this young money-lover became a disciple.

There are those who, having agreed to this, add that his discipleship was vitiated by the fact that he followed Jesus from mixed motives. He followed because he believed that Jesus was going to establish an earthly kingdom. That is true. But if you rule Judas out on this account, you will have to rule out every other member of the twelve. They all expected Jesus to establish an earthly kingdom. They did so right up to the cross. More amazing still, they cherished such expectations beyond the cross. According to the record the first question they asked the Master—and Judas was not there to prompt the asking—was this, "Lord, will you at this time restore the kingdom to Israel?" Judas therefore became a disciple, and for motives, so far as the record goes, as pure as those of any of his fellows.

3. A third fact on which we can all agree is that Judas was chosen an apostle. We read that before making this choice Jesus spent an entire night in prayer to God. Thus, after much prayer, he chose Judas. This he did not only with the consent of Judas, but of his own choice. Every disciple was not an apostle. Jesus emphasizes the fact more than once that the choice of the twelve was his very own. "You did not choose me, but I chose you." Among those thus chosen was Judas.

III

Why did Jesus choose Judas?

It was not of necessity. There were other disciples present whom Jesus might have chosen. No more did Jesus choose Judas because of ignorance. He did not understand Peter and James and John but fail to understand Judas. He knew the kind of man Judas was and what he was capable of becoming. His choice was not one of ignorance.

Nor did he choose Judas because he knew him to be a scoundrel. If I should put a man on my official board simply because I knew him to be a scoundrel, that would reflect on me. Everybody would know that my choice of one who was dishonest would indicate my own dishonesty. When Huey Long gave as his reason for appointing a certain man to a high position that said man did not have a straight bone in his body, he emphasized the crookedness of his own bones.

What is most unthinkable of all is that Judas was chosen by our Lord to do this devilish deed. If it was the will of God that Judas betray Jesus, then he is in no sense to be condemned. To live completely within the will of God, to fulfill his purpose, is perfection. If Judas was therefore sent into the world to do this deed, he is no more to blame for his treachery than was the apostle James for being the first of the twelve to be loyal even unto death.

Why, then, did Jesus choose Judas? He chose him as he did the other apostles, as a high adventure of faith. He saw the possibility of rocklike character in Simon, but Simon was anything but rock when Jesus chose him. He saw that the name of John might become a synonym for love; but when he chose John, he was so narrow and fanatical and vindictive that he was eager to call fire down from heaven and burn up certain misguided villagers who had refused himself and his Master a night's lodging. He knew what rank weeds the soul of Judas might grow. He also knew that that same fertile soil was capable of producing the loveliest of flowers. He chose Judas as he did the others, as a high adventure of faith.

IV

How, then, did Judas disappoint his Lord and become a traitor? He did not descend to those ghastly depths in a single hour or by a single bound. He went down as we do, day by day and step by step. He began his descent, I dare say, without the slightest thought or fear of the tragic end.

His descent began, I can imagine, through his disappointment. He himself did not win a place in the inner circle. That inner circle was made up of Peter and James and John. Judas was doubtless sure that he belonged in that group. He was the only man of the twelve who was not a Galilean. He was from Judea. That meant that he was in a sense from Boston, a kind of Harvard man, while his fellows were backwoodsmen from Galilee. Tradition even says that he was an aristocrat. He therefore perhaps felt himself quite superior to his fellow apostles, even to the choice three. But Jesus did not seem to share his views.

Then he came to be disappointed in Jesus himself. Judas was eager for the Master to make more rapid progress than he was making. But Jesus seemed quite dull politically. When one day enthusiasm ran high and the people desired to make him king by force, he did the unkingly thing of withdrawing and hiding himself. I am convinced that this disappointment in his own progress and in the progress of Jesus to some degree aroused his resentment.

Then, goaded by resentment and by the need of ready money, Judas one day made himself a loan from the common treasury. Of course he would soon pay it back. But for some reason he did not repay. Instead, he increased the loan. At last he persuaded himself that there was no call for him to pay it back at all. He was doing all the work. Therefore what he had taken was nothing more than a legitimate salary. This took some rationalizing. But there is no sin in which we persist that we cannot persuade ourselves is right for us, however wrong it may be for others.

Meantime his fellow apostles had not the slightest suspicion of Judas, nor did they to the very last. In the upper room when Jesus said, "One of you will betray me," we might have expected that every eye would have turned to Judas. But that was not the case. With a humility that did not always characterize them, each man looked into his own heart and said, "Lord, is it I?"

But while Judas was beyond suspicion in the eyes of his fellow apostles, there was one who knew. That one was Jesus. Judas read pain and disappointment in the eyes of his Lord. I feel sure that, in spite of his resentment, the grief of Jesus made him uncomfortable. At times he could hardly prevent himself from going to his wounded Master and pouring out his whole shameful story. But he never quite got round to it. Something always got in the way. It may have been some fancied slight that wounded his pride and roused his anger. Thus his passing grief went for nothing. He allowed the sun to go down on his anger. He allowed resentment to harden into hate. At last hate hardened into hell, and Judas became an enemy.

There are various individuals that we find easy to hate. We have a natural resentment for those who are not like ourselves. The ugly duckling early became a public enemy, not because he was really ugly, but because he was different. We find it easy to hate the folk who do not appreciate us and give us the honor to which we feel ourselves entitled. Of course we hate those who despitefully use us and persecute us. But the one we hate with greatest intensity is the one whom we have wronged, provided we are not willing to do all in our power to right that wrong.

It is easy to see why this is true. If I have wronged you and refuse to apologize, I must explain my refusal to myself. There is but one satisfactory explanation and that is that you do not deserve such an apology. To convince myself of this, I at once begin to search for the worst in you instead of for the best. Soon I am able to justify myself, for here as everywhere "he who seeks finds." Those who sought for the worst in Jesus discovered entirely to their satisfaction that he was not really a good man, but only a glutton and a drunkard and a friend of tax collectors and sinners.

Now Judas, having become a hater of Jesus, was ripe for the final blow, the betrayal. Why did those shrewd politicians who were bent on crucifying Jesus seek the services of Judas? It was not, I am sure, from necessity. There were thousands who knew Jesus. Some of these would no doubt have been glad to have pointed him out. In my opinion they used Judas because they believed it would strengthen their position to be able to say that the Master was betrayed by one of his intimate friends. Why was Judas willing thus to be used? The reason must go deeper than avarice; otherwise his method of betrayal would fail to make sense. Why the kiss when he might have stood at a distance and merely pointed his victim out? I am convinced that he was thus giving vent to his hate. His was a kiss of revenge.

V

How did Judas react? Now that the deed was done and Jesus was safe in the hands of those who were going to do him to death, how did Judas feel about it? He had fed fat the grudge he bore against him. So what? Did he then wring his hands with gleeful satisfaction? He did not. Instead, he suffered the very pangs of hell.

In his desperation he hurried to the priests, the same kind of ministers who had taught him in his childhood. In their presence he made this confession, "I have sinned in betraying innocent blood." Thus speaking, he flung down the silver on the hard mosaic floor that was even then soft as velvet in comparison with the hearts of those priests to whom he was speaking.

What response did those priests make to his appeal? They had a gospel. They knew from their Old Testament that great word,

> Though your sins are like scarlet,
> they shall be as white as snow.

But they did not give this gospel to Judas. Instead they stabbed him with a poisoned dagger: "What is that to us? See to it yourself." In all literature I know of no more hellish sentence. Yet I am afraid that I have used such language. Of course I have never said such words with my lips. But I am afraid that I have sometimes spoken them by my life as I have regarded the desperate need of others with cold indifference.

Having been jarred by this devilish word, Judas hurried away to die at the end of a rope. What was it that really wrecked Judas? It was not primarily the fact that he betrayed his Lord with a kiss, as horrible as that was. The sin that really wrecked Judas, the sin that grieved his Master more than the treacherous kiss was this: that he failed to come back and give Jesus a chance to forgive him. Judas committed the unpardonable sin. What is that sin? Not treachery, not any dark and ghastly crime. The one unpardonable sin is the refusal to accept the pardon that is offered at such cost and with such loving eagerness. If Judas had only dared to come back, he would have shown that hard by the gates of hell there is a wide-open roadway to heaven.